Transcultural Counselling

Gateways to Counselling

Consultant editor:
Windy Dryden, Professor of Counselling at Goldsmiths College, University of London

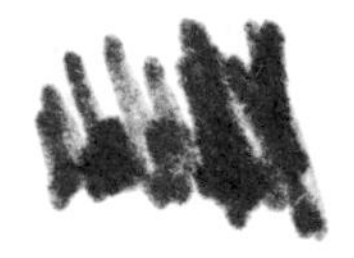

Series editor:
Maria Stasiak

Project manager:
Carron Staplehurst

The *Gateways to Counselling* series comprises books on various aspects of counselling theory and practice. Written with the assistance of the Central School of Counselling and Therapy, one of the largest counselling training organisations in the UK, the books address the needs of both students and tutors and are relevant for a range of training courses, regardless of specific orientation.

Other books in the series include:

STARVING TO LIVE
The paradox of anorexia nervosa
Alessandra Lemma-Wright

AN INTRODUCTION TO CO-DEPENDENCY FOR COUNSELLORS
Gill Reeve

COUNSELLING SKILLS FOR PROFESSIONAL HELPERS
John Pratt

COUNSELLING IN A GENERAL PRACTICE SETTING
James Breese

ON LISTENING AND LEARNING
Student counselling in further and higher education
Colin Lago and Geraldine Shipton

TRANSCULTURAL COUNSELLING

Zack Eleftheriadou

Central Book Publishing Ltd
London

First published 1994
by Central Book Publishing Ltd
Centre House, 56B Hale Lane
London, NW7 3PR

Phototypeset in 10 on 12 point Century Roman and Optima by
Intype, London
Printed in Great Britain by
Tudor Printing, Park Road, Barnet

Cover illustration by Helen S. Roper

British Library Cataloguing in Publication Data

Eleftheriadou, Zack
Transcultural Counselling. – (Gateways
to Counselling Series)
I. Title II. Series
361.323

ISBN 1–898458–20–0

Contents

Acknowledgements

I would like to thank my editors, Maria Stasiak and Windy Dryden for their invaluable advice and hard work throughout the development of the book; it was especially helpful to have Maria's enthusiasm in the project. I would like to thank Dr Ernesto Spinelli, who originally supervised this project as an MA thesis, for his constant support with my work over the last nine years. I would like to thank the late Founder and Director of Nafsiyat, Jafar Kareem, for placing the whole area of cross-cultural counselling on the counselling field map. His work will always be remembered and I thank him for his encouragement with my projects. I would also like to express my appreciation to Dr Suman Fernando as well as the rest of the Race and Culture Study Group at Chase Farm Hospital, Enfield and the BAC division of Race and Cultural Education in Counselling (RACE) Committee for the many difficult issues we have struggled with during our meetings, which have been an important part of my self-development as a therapist. I would also like to express my sincere gratitude to the clients and students who have allowed me into their cultures and who continue to educate me and challenge my ideas.

On a more personal note, I would like to thank Michelle Cohen for her patience in reading the manuscript and advising me on necessary changes. I would like to express my thanks to my colleagues Alessandra Lemma-Wright, Liza Romish-Clay, Brett Kahr, Hideo Ikehara and Biddy Arnott for their faith in the project and for the many fruitful (and lengthy!) discussions we have engaged in regarding this book. I would like to extend a special thank you to Hideo for allowing me to publish the fascinating case study of the Vietnamese client (see Chapter 5). Lastly, but most certainly not least, I would like to thank my parents who have always been my most consistent support and who have taught me the importance of my own roots as well as of learning and respecting those of different cultural backgrounds.

Introduction

The writing of this book is a reflection of my own experience of living in different parts of the world – Cyprus, Saudi Arabia and Britain – going through the Greek-Cypriot, Greek, British and American educational systems, and also of the invaluable interaction over the years with international colleagues and friends. Additionally and most importantly, my thoughts on this area are derived from counselling children and adults from West Africa, North America, South America, Australia, England, Ireland, Scotland, Israel, Cyprus, Germany, Greece, Holland, India, Pakistan, the Philippines, Iraq and the West Indies. The exposure to these cultures has, at times, been a positive reinforcement to my own Greek-Cypriot cultural values and beliefs and has at other times created an internal conflict. Overall, the process (which is always ongoing) of integrating all the different cultures I have experienced has been of enormous value in attempting to understand and accept those who are racially/culturally different, in my counselling and teaching work as well as in my personal life.

Chapter 1 is a detailed account of what we mean by *race, culture* and *ethnicity* and of how they relate to transcultural counselling. The distinction is a necessary one as they are terms with different meanings, but which have often been used interchangeably.

Chapter 2 is an introduction to and general overview of the factors which contributed to the birth and expansion of the cross-cultural counselling field. This includes the important influence of psychology on counselling theory and practice and the increasing involvement of ethnic minorities in the field of cross-cultural counselling, both as clients and as therapists.

These changes have resulted in dramatic changes in cross-cultural counselling practice.

Chapter 3 introduces the different barriers we encounter in transcultural counselling. There are numerous examples of the variety of communication and behaviour patterns between different cultures which illustrate potential misunderstandings that may occur.

Chapter 4 introduces a framework for working with cultural issues, based on the theory and practice of existential/phenomenological analysis and some elements from psychoanalytic theory, such as transference and countertransference. This philosophical base is useful, first because it recognises that counsellors and clients from different cultures have adopted different worldviews. Secondly, it is essential for the counsellor to have examined his or her own philosophy of life. Both participants are seen as equal in the therapeutic relationship, rather than one being an expert and one a layperson. Clinical material is used throughout to illustrate specific instances in therapeutic practice where the transcultural framework was used.

Chapter 5 identifies the clients most likely to enter cross-cultural counselling and the problems they are likely to experience. The chapter includes many case studies that demonstrate the importance of taking into consideration both external cultural/ethnic elements, such as racism, as well as individual aspects of the clients' experience.

Chapter 6 gives a general overview of the book and provides some suggestions for research and counselling practice in the cross-cultural field.

1

Defining Culture

> Society exists for the benefit of its members: not the members for the benefit of society.
>
> (Herbert Spencer)

In this chapter, the concept of culture will be defined, followed by an explanation of why it is particularly important to take culture as a system into account when dealing with clients from different racial and cultural backgrounds. The important distinction between culture, race and ethnicity will be made. A detailed study then follows of how an individual becomes socialised into a certain culture.

The words cross-cultural and intercultural are used interchangeably throughout the book, to describe research and theoretical material and counselling practice across different cultures; the word transcultural is used to refer to a specific counselling framework that *considers* culture, but *goes beyond* it.

In cross-cultural counselling, it is important to understand the relationship between the individual and culture in order to engage in the counselling process effectively. It is taken as a basic premise in this book that an individual develops within a context or cultural milieu. The first task is therefore to define what exactly is meant by *culture*.

WHAT IS CULTURE?

Culture is a way of creating shared ways of functioning in order to communicate effectively, without which it would be virtually impossible for a large group of people to operate as a whole. In order to communicate, we create shared events, practices, roles, values, myths, rules, beliefs, habits, symbols, illusions and realities. For instance, we talk of the rituals of 'religious ceremonies' or a 'wedding'.

The concept of culture can be used to describe a whole country, an ethnic group within a large country – for example, the Palestinian Arabs in Israel – or it can be used to refer to sub-groups, such as the socio-economic classes in Britain. Culture refers to the shared ways of behaving for those who belong to a certain society. It is a social construction of the non-physical aspects of the environment. It used to be thought of as something static that existed externally of the person, but it is now seen as dynamic, always changing, influenced by and influencing the individual. In other words, it exists inside people (psychologically) and outside (in the existing social institutions). These two aspects are constantly in interaction and in flux.

Culture has objective characteristics and subjective characteristics. Objective characteristics are visible and physical, such as roads, buildings and the whole environmental landscape (Shweder 1991). Subjective characteristics are abstract, like roles and belief systems. These beliefs and ideas are learnt and shared from generation to generation and transmitted through the process of socialisation. The key people in this process are usually our parents and teachers; in some cultures, like Arab, Southern European or Eastern cultures, elders also play an important role. Cultural information is like a flexible dictionary which is handed down and which gives the appropriate cultural definition of every single event, object or concept. Transmission is more subtle for the abstract aspects than it is for the concrete aspects. Thus, learning the values and ideas of a culture is less overt than learning the cultural dress codes, diet, language or ways of participating in ceremonies.

Culture is not a rigid or closed system of ideas. It is a flexible construction of the world to which a certain group of people belong, which is geographically and historically specific. It changes with each generation, as well as with the influx of others or exposure to other cultural constructions.

CULTURE, RACE AND ETHNICITY

Although the concepts of culture, race and ethnicity are often used interchangeably, we need to define them accurately as they do not mean the same thing. By distinguishing between these concepts and looking at individual's relationship with these aspects of the psycho-social environment, we become aware of how influential they can be in our images of other people. Fernando (1991) is one of the few clinicians who has quite clearly distinguished between culture, race and ethnicity, in his highly informative book *Mental Health, Race and Culture*. Generally speaking, Fernando defines culture as a sociological construction, race as relating to the physical aspects of the environment and ethnicity as a primarily psychological state.

Race

A race is defined as a group of people who have the same skin colour, hair shape and colour, eye colour and blood type, and a common ancestry. Unfortunately, historical ideas about race still persist, despite the fact that there is little evidence for actual genetic differences between races. Scientifically, race is an invalid concept and research has shown that there are more differences within one racial group than between racial groups. More importantly, there is no evidence that any one race is 'pure', since we all belong to pluralistic societies. The term 'race' has been used, and is still being used, to discriminate against groups of people who differ in skin colour. It is also used incorrectly to refer to people who do not differ in skin colour, for example Jewish people, making them appear as a distinctly different group with rigid characteristics. It can be used to classify racial groups into hierarchical categories, so that some groups are seen as inferior and others as superior. When people are classified into groups they are no longer viewed as individuals. Western Europe has a long history of classifying people according to their race. Often the racial label has been implied through the use of less overt terminology. In Britain, Africans, West Indians, Asians and Cypriots used to be called 'immigrants'. Generally, the terms 'immigrants' or 'New Commonwealth immigrants' were (and in some contexts) still are used for all the 'brown/black-skinned' ethnic groups and were not applied to white immigrants. Nowadays, immigrants are called *ethnic minorities*, an attempt to break away from the defining characteristic of skin colour and to encompass the European and other 'white' immigrants. However, the term 'ethnic minorities' is used by some to label the black immigrants. Each new term which comes into use becomes loaded with its own connotations (Littlewood and Lipsedge 1989).

Ethnicity

Both 'race' and 'culture' are now being replaced by the concept of ethnicity. A group who share a specific history, background or origin, and who have a common culture are said to form an ethnic group. Ethnicity is related to a basic psychological need for a sense of belonging and collectiveness. This is reinforced by social pressures on people to belong to a particular national group. Factors such as a shared nationality, language, religion, race or physical appearance (or both of these) may form a bond between people. For example, if a person feels that he or she is part of the Asian culture it implies that this is an important element of his or her psychological identity. The person may practice one particular religion or language of the Asian culture, but there is a strong identification with what being 'Asian' represents.

Ethnicity is not a clear-cut grouping; because it is a psychological state and because it is seen as 'potentially changeable and assimilable' (Fernando 1991: 20) it is a far more flexible concept than race. It is prone to social influences, unlike race, which is defined biologically, and is thus unchangeable. In a racist society, the word ethnic may be used inaccurately to refer to racial characteristics rather than changeable ethnic or cultural characteristics. This often results in the creation of conflict or stress because it becomes a rigid label.

THE RELATIONSHIP BETWEEN THE INDIVIDUAL AND CULTURE

According to the existential/phenomenological view (see Deurzen-Smith 1988, Spinelli 1989), from the moment of birth we begin the uniquely human endeavour of trying to find meaning for the behaviour of others, and trying to find significance in the events or objects in our environment and in everything that goes on in the world around us. The world is full of possibilities and experiences we can engage in, but as individuals, we form our own interpretation and understanding. Our perception is a subjective construction of the world, since information about the world has been interpreted through unique beliefs, expectations and past experiences. There is no doubt that there is also an external reality which exists independently of us but is not universal, since we do not actually experience the world as it is, but as we interpret it. When we speak of 'reality' or of the 'objective world' we therefore mean the active interaction between 'external' or social events and our own perception of them.

The individual and his or her culture are intertwined. They influence each other and make up each other's subsequent identity. It is not a static relationship, as the subjective or intrapsychic world can be altered through exposure to the socio-cultural environment. The meanings we attribute to behaviours and actions are formulated and changed according to the way socio-cultural messages are interpreted. The messages may come from the political system, the media, our family unit or other important social institutions. When they alter, we react accordingly, by choosing to review our formulations (values, beliefs and ideas) or change them completely. Similarly, the socio-cultural world is active in that its ideas and practices do not remain static. On the contrary, the ideas are constantly changing and taking new ideas into consideration. For example, trends or practices from other cultures can be influential and over time can be adopted. As long there is a community of people with beliefs and ideas, we are constantly interacting with that community, and subsequently being influenced by and influencing it. It is vital for those engaged in counselling practice to keep in mind that these elements cannot be analysed independently; each one must be defined in relation to the other.

The implicit assumption made is, therefore, that we are dynamic beings who have, to an extent, the ability to influence and eventually change our environment. This is directly relevant to therapeutic practice; without it, therapy would be purposeless. In every instance, human beings have a choice in how they face life situations. Yet those choices have to be made within an already historically and socially created world, full of uncertainties and limitations, which people must be flexible enough to deal with. The client must become aware of the paradoxes of life and accept them.

Socialisation into a culture can become a rigid and inauthentic process. We all go through socialisation and obtain certain cues about the direction that is expected of us. If these cues are used in a fixed way and we expect them always to stay that way, we place ourselves in an extremely restricted position. This is a passive way of accepting culturally prescribed roles and denies our freedom and our responsibility for our existence and relationship to the world. It can place us in a position of *inauthenticity,* or not being true to ourselves. It is a distorted and unreal relationship, which depersonalises the individual. In other words, the person can be out of touch with what he or she really feels, thinks and values. Departing from the inauthentic does not necessarily mean rejecting society and living in solitude. One can feel authentic as an individual and also feel a genuine sense of community. This occurs when one is part of a group, but manages also to be true to oneself; not playing a rigid or restrictive role in the group, but relating to others as a whole person. Authenticity also implies a responsibility to oneself and to those we live with in that world for the choices made. Whenever individuals choose a course of action, they are not only choosing what they will do, but are also choosing to some extent for those around them. Choice is not to be taken to the extreme in the sense that people have to go through life making choices and decisions in every possible area of their life. Total choice is not completely possible because we do not exist in isolation; whichever culture or sub-culture we belong to, we will always be influenced by it and influence it.

MODES OF RELATING TO THE WORLD

In order to comprehend how an individual's experience of the world is created, it will broken down into artificial components; each one will be examined in turn. In reality, these sub-parts – the *Umwelt, Eigenwelt* and *Mitwelt* (Binswanger 1968; Boss 1963) and the *Uberwelt* (Deurzen-Smith 1988) – are all interconnected to form the person's experience of the world. We can use the four components to study human psycho-social development because people cope with the different dimensions in different ways.

The *Umwelt* refers to the natural world or environment. This could be the physical environment and hence physical space the person is used to; for example living in the countryside is a totally different experience of physical space compared to a densely built city environment. It is the meaning of this physical world *to the person* which has to be identified.

The *Mitwelt* refers to the public or interpersonal world of the individual. The Mitwelt includes all of the person's significant human relationships, interactions and support systems, which are largely culturally defined. It is the sphere where the most intimate interactions take place and is usually the most influential. It consists of the individual's relationship to race, ethnicity and social stratification (the person's relationship to his or her class, parent's social class or any other reference group); his or her family and peers and how they are involved with the individual; and finally, the role the individual plays within the family group or peer group.

On a macro-scale, the Mitwelt includes various other elements. The organisational element consists of the different organisations the individual may belong to. It includes relationships with superiors and subordinates, and the degree of influence of these individual organisations. The occupational element of the person includes the type of work environment he or she is involved with (e.g. working in a group or in isolation), the degree of support at work and his or her career pattern. The community group consists of the type of community the person belongs to, the degree of support the individual gains from it and the type of interactions which take place in this area, as well as the individual's involvement with or isolation from it. Other broader societal issues include his or her general attitude towards authority and the law, religion, economics and politics, etc.

Social groups, such as the family, peers, organisations, etc., both across cultures and within cultures, have shared belief systems, similar patterns of interaction and similar notions of what is normal or appropriate behavioural/emotional expression. But although some generally shared ideas and beliefs can be found in the inner world of clients of the same ethnicity, age, gender, biographical experience and social background, there will also be different interpretations of the world.

All the aspects of the Mitwelt and the individual's culture are integrated uniquely by the individual to form the *Eigenwelt*. The Eigenwelt is the private, intrapersonal, intimate aspect of the person. It is how the individual feels or perceives himself or herself within the environment; it is to do with self-image, personal identity and personal beliefs and value systems. A counsellor can be most helpful in aiding the client to discover his or her individual essence.

The *Uberwelt* refers to the abstract, spiritual aspect of the individual; that which is beyond himself or herself. It is the individual's ideological outlook on life, the aspirations, ideals, morals, beliefs and values he or she holds about life; for example, for some people this ideology may be religion or transcendental experiences. The Uberwelt is unique to the individual because it has been uniquely constructed and is deeply meaningful only to the individual. For many people this aspect of their life remains relatively unknown.

These four modes of relating are in constant interaction to create the person's *worldview* (see Figure 1). This is a concept encompassing status, experiences, attitudes and expectations, skills, knowledge, beliefs, values and lifestyle, as well as one's particular relationship to the world, other people, institutions and physical aspects of the world.

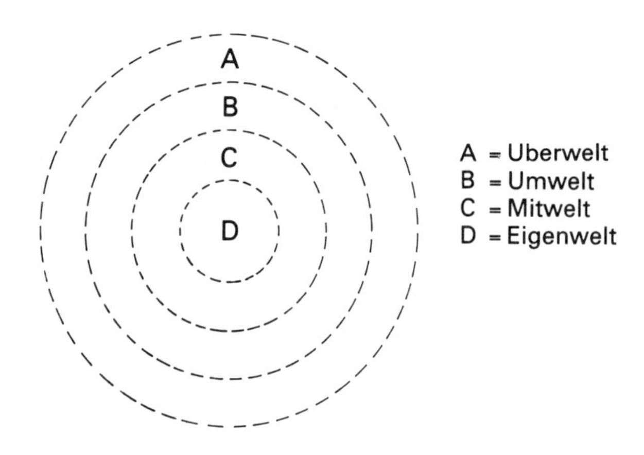

Figure 1 The modes of relating

The circles shown in the diagram are not closed because each has enough permeability to infiltrate material into the others and to be infiltrated by them. When they become experienced as closed circles it is because people's experience of *being-in-the-world* becomes restricted and suffocating. These modes provide us with a helpful way of examining the total experience of the client during counselling. The modes of relating can be seen as the personal or individual identity, the social or group identity, the physical and the spiritual or panhuman. Problems or conflicts are likely to take place when one of the modes becomes extremely disturbed and then it is likely that the person will seek help. In my experience, the person is usually unclear about which mode is creating the problem, but he or she knows something is 'static' and confusing and external assistance is sought to try and create a psychological change.

DISCUSSION ISSUES

1 Using your own experiences identify (1) your own race, ethnicity and culture and (2) how people from a different culture may define your race, ethnicity and culture, particularly those you meet for the first time. Do the views differ?

2 Outline your own worldview through the four modes of relating, highlighting the fundamental values, beliefs and attitudes of each area.

2

Counselling Across Cultures

> Each man must invent his own values, and he exists authentically in so far as he strives to realise values that are really his own.
>
> (Jean-Paul Sartre)

In this chapter the focus will be on the reasons why cross-cultural counselling was formulated as a category distinct from other counselling approaches. Different types of cultures and psychological theories of culture will be outlined and the impact they have had on counselling theory and practice will be analysed. The western notion of counselling will be contrasted to that of other cultures, focusing on the ways each defines 'problem' or 'disturbance'.

REASONS FOR THE RECENT RISE AND EXPANSION OF CROSS-CULTURAL COUNSELLING

The sub-discipline of cross-cultural therapy has existed for many years, in a number of forms, such as *vergleichende psychiatrie* or comparative psychiatry, primitive psychiatry, culture and psychopathology, ethnopsychiatry, transcultural psychiatry, cross-cultural psychiatry and many others (see Marsella 1979). It is not until recently, however, that the field has gained credibility and as a result has grown rapidly. There are many reasons for the expansion; the increasing mobility of people which has increased cultural pluralism, the European Community's amalgamation in 1992 which has imposed certain guidelines for training of counsellors, the position of ethnic minorities and changes in the field of psychology and consequently psychological research.

In recent years there has been a growing awareness of the cultural pluralism of western countries like America, France and Britain. In the United States, for example, 20 per cent of the population consists of ethnic minority immigrants from countries like Cuba, Japan, Indo-China and Africa. Ethnic minority immigrants make up 5 per cent of the population in Britain, with immigrants from India, Pakistan, West Indies, Africa, Cyprus and Ireland, amongst other nations.

Despite cultural pluralism, different ethnic groups continue to face social, political, educational and economic disadvantage and discrimination. In both the United States and Britain, riots and conflicts have highlighted, time and time again, the problems faced by different ethnic groups. In the United States, ethnic minorities are inappropriately served by the existing mental health services (Sue and Zane 1987). For example, ethnic groups such as American Indians, Asian Americans, Blacks and Hispanics represent 20 per cent of the population in the US and yet this is not reflected in the mental health services uptake. In Britain, there is only some research and clinical evidence (e.g. Khan 1991) to show that the counselling/psychology services do not reflect this racial and cultural diversity. Therefore, it is difficult to prove this pattern across Britain, as very few counselling centres publish figures regarding the racial and cultural backgrounds of clients and most of the existing research has tended to focus on psychiatric patients. In Britain, ethnic minority clients are more likely to be psychiatrically diagnosed as 'mentally disturbed' than members of the majority western population (Fernando 1991) and there is some evidence that they are more likely to be given higher dosages of drugs and electro-convulsive therapy (Littlewood and Lipsedge 1989). Indeed, this trend seems to be on the increase, which is cause for great concern. Although ethnic minorities make up a large proportion of the psychiatric clientele (as opposed to the clients who enter counselling) few members of ethnic minorities train as mental health workers.

Even when mental health professionals have tried to take possible cultural factors into consideration, it has been found that clients from ethnic minority groups have significantly higher dropout rates during therapy than the white population

(Lowenstein 1987). In fact, Lowenstein found that half of the ethnic minority clients in his sample did not return to therapy after the first session, whilst only 30 per cent of the white population did not return. It is still unclear why this trend exists, but some of the reasons may be the following: clients have been found to be 'unmotivated, resistant and lacking in psychological mindedness' (Pedersen *et al.* 1989: 5); many ethnic minority clients are not aware of the existing mental health services, and many do not understand them or value them as helpful; from the professionals' point of view, ethnic minority clients are considered 'difficult' cases to deal with, because they have different, sometimes meaningless, backgrounds to the majority culture or are considered to be unfamiliar and thus non-compliant to the western 'culture' of counselling. In addition, in most cases ethnic minority clients are not seen as priority clients because their problems are not considered to be as important as those of clients who belong to the majority culture. This can be attributed to ignorance about other cultures' practices and language, and the prejudices and racism of western mental health professionals, that people from other cultures, particularly from some races, are inferior.

It is as important that professionals' attitudes change as it is to change policies and have on-going monitoring of the uptake of services. Usually counsellors prefer to work with those who share similar attributes. This may be because it is generally easier to communicate with and be understood by someone of a similar cultural background; outsiders may be perceived as threatening because they are different. Most therapists do not have a knowledge of other cultures and their professional training is appropriate only for the majority population. There is generally little or no training offered for professionals working with cross-cultural issues. For example, in the United States there are only about fifteen training centres in this field (Moses 1990). It has normally been expected that foreigners should adjust to the norms and values of the host country (Lowenstein 1987).

Generally, the influence of culture has been underestimated, especially in the field of counselling. In Britain, for example, there has been almost no research in the field. However, in the last two decades, due to the growing awareness of racial/

cultural pluralism, psychologists have shown an interest in the relationship between human behaviour, emotion and culture, and hence there has been a growing number of intercultural meetings and communications. If the whole field of cross-cultural counselling is really to cater for the needs of the racially or culturally different client, it is necessary for counsellors to understand other cultural practices beyond their own cultural group.

This new area of interest has also been highlighted because of the new legislation being enforced in the therapy field, with the merging of the European Community in 1992. This legislation has developed equivalency training levels for mental health professionals, in order for culturally different trainings to be acceptable across Europe. In addition, the increasing assertiveness of minority groups (especially evident in the United States), has resulted in ethnic minority groups taking a much more active role in counselling theory and practice. These groups are important because they can provide informative lectures or workshops that can give us an insight into a completely new culture. At times it may also be necessary for more bilingual/bicultural people to become involved with counsellors for interpreting purposes. In Britain, for example, organisations such as the intercultural therapy centre Nafsiyat, which offers consultations, therapy, seminars and workshops; the Transcultural Psychiatry Society; the British Association for Counselling division of Race and Cultural Education in Counselling (RACE); the British Psychological Society sub-section of race and culture; as well as telephone helplines such as the Haringey Multi-Ethnic Helpline (Advocacy) Project, have a high percentage of ethnic minority members. Most professionals now realise that cultural factors have been neglected, and this has had an impact on theory, research and practice. Most of the literature in the cross-cultural field has emerged in the last decade, especially the last two to three years. Nowadays, counselling books show a growing professional awareness of cultural issues. *Aliens and Alienists* by Littlewood and Lipsedge, *Transcultural Counselling in Action* by d'Ardenne and Mahtani, *Mental Health, Race and Culture* by Fernando and *Intercultural Therapy* by Kareem and Littlewood (see References) are a few good instances of this trend. The discipline of psychology has also started to take cultural issues into consideration (see below). This is evident in many associations, such as the American Psychological Association, which since 1982 has included a section on cross-cultural aspects of psychology. There have also been major research projects on the concepts used in cross-cultural counselling. Theories have been re-examined and broadened, and implications for practice have been considered.

Recently, the number of ethnic minority groups entering clinical and counselling training programmes in the United States has been on the increase. Similarly in Britain, there is a growing awareness of the need for more specialised training in the cross-cultural counselling field. In the past, knowledge of other cultures was so abstract that its implications could not be translated directly into the clinical therapeutic situation. The connection between theory and practice is gradually being taken more seriously by researchers and trainers. This has resulted in more meaningful and effective ways of working with ethnic minority groups.

PSYCHOLOGICAL THEORIES OF CULTURE

A major contributing factor to the advances in cross-cultural counselling practice has been changes within the field of psychology. Cross-cultural psychology has been developed as a sub-branch of psychology, with the aim of considering cultural aspects of the emotions and behaviour of individuals and groups. Much of the research within this field has examined western concepts in different cultures, for example examining the western psychiatric terms of depression and schizophrenia across cultures. Usually the research has been conducted by western professionals from an outsider's point of view of the different cultures. This has caused stereotypes of other cultures and gross misunderstandings of cultural behaviours to be reinforced. This was more evident in the past, where non-western cultures were labelled as 'primitive'. Thus, individuals from non-western cultures were thought to have reached a lower level of cognitive development compared with those of western cultures. The work of the developmental theorist Piaget was meant to illustrate these differences and in the United States Jensen claimed that IQ tests showed that blacks were less intelligent than whites. He attributed this to genetic factors. Similarly, the behaviour of ethnic minorities which did not match middle-class mainstream American white culture was attributed to social disadvantage or social deprivation. Both *genetic* and *cultural deficit* models have now been dismissed in favour of the *culturally different* models (Sue and Sue 1981). These imply that cultures are different, but not inferior or superior because of the difference. The key words in any cross-cultural work are indeed 'difference' and 'variation', in experiences, emotional expression and behaviour of people.

Nowadays, some professionals within the counselling field seem to share the same basic premise as cross-cultural psychology; that all mental processes and behaviour are universal and that underneath the 'layer' of culture all people are the same. Therefore, it is believed that culture distorts similarities, but that once this layer is eliminated universal characteristics emerge. This view was questioned during the late 1980s, with the growth of the new sub-discipline of *cultural psychology*. The rise of cultural psychology has been a step forward, because it has acknowledged that not all behaviour and emotion is necessarily universal. It has been an attempt to break away from the basic psychology principle of the psychic unity of humankind. In this book it is assumed that culture is more than just a removable 'layer'. The individual is so deeply ingrained in his or her culture that it cannot be ignored. In counselling it is important to take account of the individual's culture and to try to understand how we create the meaning of our own world within it. In doing so, we can begin to understand how the socio-cultural world can have a bearing on the way we view our world and can subsequently influence the way we act, think and feel in it.

It is important to take both cross-cultural psychology and cultural psychology into consideration, as some behaviours may be found to be similar in different cultures and others may not. If nothing was similar across cultures then cross-cultural communication would be impossible, so we do need comparison of our concepts with other cultures. At the same time there are undoubtedly many differences across cultures that cannot be taken out of their context and be understood.

IDEOLOGICAL ROOTS OF COUNSELLING

The underutilisation of mental health services by ethnic minority clients and the lack of 'success' of western therapists with non-western clients seem to persist because clients are viewed from a western viewpoint. The fact that throughout history every culture has had its own way of providing support and psychological help for people in distress has not been considered. For example, food-gathering societies such as the !Kung Bushmen of the Kalahari Desert in Southwest Africa tend to heal through magic or supernatural methods; more complex fishing-gathering societies, such as the Shui-jen or water people of Southern China (Lenski and Lenski 1982) practise medical or religious types of therapy; agricultural and industrialised societies (these include societies which have been or are currently being influenced by industrialisation) have modern counselling methods which include behaviour therapy, psychoanalysis, humanistic or existential therapies and cognitive therapy or psychiatry.

Every approach is embedded in its own culture, with its own guidelines on what is normal or abnormal, how reality is interpreted, what the values of that culture are and what standards and conduct have to be followed. The basic assumptions of any type of healing work are a direct product of their culture of origin. Draguns (1974) points out how the Protestant ethic is evident in the scientific, rational approach to western counselling and psychology and in how active participation by individuals is encouraged. Counselling is a twentieth-century, white, bourgeois, Euro-American construction. It is a concept that encompasses salient American features such as individualism, egalitarianism, social mobility and change (Khan 1991). Western counselling is identified with four general assumptions: that the client's problems are intrapsychic (taking place within the person); that the appropriate therapeutic approach is also intrapsychic; that clients are familiar with the counsellor–client relationship, the process and the whole 'culture' of counselling; and that the 'talking cure' is effective (Smith 1985). In the United States, for example, client-centred therapy is very popular because it emphasises the importance of the individual. It holds implicit beliefs that the individual is responsible, and has choice and freedom in his or her own life. However, in many other cultures this would be unacceptable because one grows up valuing the communal more than the individual. In the United States, individuals are encouraged to disclose information during therapy; this is discouraged in other cultures, such as Southern European countries or in the Middle East. In China, for example, Chinese divination or folk counselling is used, which encourages conservatism and discourages ambition and aggression. In Japan, Naikan therapy or introspection therapy is practised, a type of therapy originating from Buddhist philosophy which involves meditation and self-introspection. It reflects the importance of the social, especially familial morals of Japanese society. In later chapters, the basic premises of western counselling will be questioned and the social (as opposed to the psychic) aspects of behaviour will be considered.

Here, the concept of counselling is used to cover a range of psychological work with clients, whether it is a short-term and focused or long-term and more open-ended counselling process. The terms 'counselling' and 'therapy' will be used interchangeably in later chapters.

DISCUSSION ISSUES

1 Do you think the sub-discipline of cross-cultural counselling is a necessary one?

2 What is your philosophy of counselling? Do you think your own counselling framework is applicable across cultures?

3

Barriers to Cross-Cultural Counselling

Beauty is in the eye of the beholder.
(Margaret Wolfe Hungerford)

In this chapter, specific problems arising when counselling clients from different cultures will be discussed. I will examine whether behaviour and emotional expression, concept formation and manifestation of disturbance are universal or culture-specific and how different types of cultures differ in societal roles, social groups, emotional expressiveness, etc. Where cross-cultural variation has been found clinical practice vignettes will be referred to for illustration.

UNIVERSAL OR CULTURE-SPECIFIC?

'Normality' versus 'abnormality'

An issue which has been controversial for many years is what constitutes a 'problem' or 'psychological disturbance'. In working with a client, there must be some criteria we can refer to which defines what is appropriate and what is inappropriate behaviour and emotion. It is difficult to find agreement about these criteria even among therapists of the same culture.

Are definitions of what is *healthy* or *normal* versus *disturbed* or *abnormal* culturally specific or are these concepts universal? In this book, the term 'psychological problem' is used to denote any form of psychological conflict a person may experience that interferes with his or her daily life, but that still allows him or her to cope. A psychological problem is defined by an individual's as well as his or her sub-cultural and cultural milieu's concept of health/distress. For a different culture counsellor it is important to distinguish the cultural elements from the individual elements. The term 'disturbance' is used to mean an extreme form of psychological conflict, where the person suffering may be unable to function and as a result begins to neglect him or herself, does not eat, engages in behaviour that is considered 'bizarre' by his or her family and/or cultural group, etc.

But is normality or abnormality a result of biological or psycho-social factors, or both? There are generally three different views held by professionals. The first is that all types of psychological problems/disturbance are the same in form and expression across cultures because they are biologically defined. The second view is that a problem/disturbance has biological roots which interact with cultural elements and this leads to variation of conditions. A third view is that culturally-specific problems/disturbances exist, implying that they are formed as a result of a particular socio-cultural context and thus cannot be found in other cultures. Many such conditions have been identified, such as the states of *amok, susto, latah, witiko* and *koro*, which have been described only in certain countries (see Leff 1988 and Berry *et al.* 1992). There is a growing tendency nowadays to take the view that disturbance may have either biological or socio-cultural roots, or both. Where both biological and social factors are interlinked the person may be more susceptible to becoming disturbed.

Research has shown that clients from different cultures do present similar psychological and behavioural symptoms, but whether they are the same type of psychological problems or disturbances still remains unclear. This finding is not surprising, because when we try to apply western diagnostic categories to other cultures we immediately fall into problems of equivalency in meaning. For example, according to the western diagnostic categories, one of the symptoms of disturbance is hallucinations or hearing voices. However, in India hearing voices can be a sign of a 'guru', or one who has been blessed. Another instance is prophecy in dreams, which is commonly reported by Greeks and West Indians. A West Indian client was hesitant to report a dream during counselling because she believed that if it was verbalised it would come true. Another example is of an extremely religious Cypriot client who reported proudly that she was named after a spiritual figure; 'an angel came into [her mother's] dream' whilst her mother was pregnant. She saw this as a blessing, rather than something that implied any type of disturbance in her or her mother because they believed this to be true. If this is reported to a psychiatrist among a series of statements that were totally foreign and meaningless, the mental health professional would have to exercise caution in making a diagnosis. It is essential to analyse clients' statements according to their corresponding cultural context (see Littlewood and Lipsedge 1989).

The subject of whether disturbance is universal or culture-specific, however, remains controversial with the professionals (see Leff 1988), because western diagnosis may label a condition as a symptom of disturbance because it has similar features across cultures. However, it does not necessarily mean the condition is the same cross-culturally when it is examined in depth. For example, when certain psychiatric conditions are compared, such as hyperactivity in children, there are differences in prevalence rates depending on the different ways behaviours are interpreted. When studies are conducted by researchers of the same culture as the population studied it has been found that the prevalence rates are more similar across cultures. It is difficult to separate the aspects which are similar as the expression and meaning of the condition is culturally defined. Simply trying to compare a type of disturbance across cultures, from outside of those cultures, places the object out of its context. This can render it meaningless to the outsider, and make it open to any interpretation. One should question whether some of the 'exotic' conditions described through cross-cultural research are not just cases which simply do not fit into the western psychiatric categories. We would not do justice to the complexity of the problem by beginning to unfold here the problems one encounters in studying this area. What is important is to be open to variations in behaviour and emotional expression across cultures. Even when culturally different behavioural patterns appear to fit the western notion of disturbance, it is best to exercise caution in labelling them as such.

Concepts

The meanings of concepts in everyday usage can often be taken for granted when interacting with someone from the same cultural group. When we encounter someone from outside of our culture it becomes necessary to step back from our familiar meaning and discover how other cultures may define concepts. In Chinese there is only one word for 'anxiety', 'tension' and 'worry' (Leff 1988). In the Indian language there is no word for the western notion of 'guilt'. Instead there are words for 'criminal' behaviour, which to a western counsellor would convey a completely different picture. These examples demonstrate the importance of language in understanding concepts. The failure to understand can lead to profound misinterpretation and subsequent frustration for the client. In their illuminating book, *Aliens and Alienists* (1989), Littlewood and Lipsedge discuss the comparatively higher admission rates for schizophrenia for West Indian and West African clients. This has been attributed to British psychiatrists' misinterpreting language and behaviour. Psychiatric diagnosis is especially vulnerable to misinterpretations, because diagnostic categories do not take into consideration the cultural meaning of a given behaviour.

Manifestation of problems

Each culture has approved ways in which distress can be expressed and demonstrated. In the West, it is assumed that problems should be discussed through talk of the mind, or *psychologisation*. In many other countries however, problems are expressed through talk of the body, or through *somatisation*. For example, in the Yoruba language, it is difficult to find equivalents for the commonly used western words 'depression' and 'anxiety'. Instead, Yoruba people refer to these concepts through bodily states, such as 'the heart is weak' or 'the heart is not at rest'. However, there is inadequate research as yet to prove that the mode of emotional expression is culturally bound. Even if there are cultural similarities clients will, undoubtedly, have their own preferred mode of emotional expression

DIFFERENT TYPES OF CULTURES

Cultural variations will undoubtedly influence the counselling interaction and the expectations of the client and the counsellor. In this section, the different values and beliefs will be divided into two basic cultural types: the individualistic and the collectivist (Triandis 1990). Examples of the former are most western countries, like the United States and Britain. Examples of the latter are the Southern European, South American and East Asian cultures, which are regionally collectivist. Although the definitions of the two types of cultures are extreme and superficial in that they only broadly describe cultural patterns it is useful to examine these two in terms of the different behaviour patterns their members present.

In individualist cultures, there is emphasis on self-goals, wishes and needs and there is less influence from groups. The individual is encouraged to be self-reliant rather than group-reliant. If the needs of the individual are different from the needs of the group there is more flexibility to leave it and pursue one's own needs. Different social groups can be formed at the discretion of the individual. The individual chooses which people to socialise with. In collectivist cultures, there are groups of people that one must associate with, for example family members. Thus, there is more independence in the former group whilst in the latter interdependence is encouraged. Similarly, not all cultures share the European and American emphasis on individuality, individual competition, written traditions, linear time and youth. Africans, for example, who have a more collective society, place a high value on the communal, place a higher value on learning from elders than on written information and have a different organisation of time. In the collectivist cultural system, subordination to the family and generally, to the collective, is encouraged; autonomy is discouraged and perceived as an obstacle (Kakar 1990). In collectivist cultures, individuals do not influence society as much as the group does. It is evident that in some countries the state is very influential in art, religion, politics, science and many other aspects of everyday life. In this case, the political system is a reinforcing factor for a collectivist type of society, because it does not allow for non-conformity. Collectivism is thus encouraged on a national level, rather than on a community or family scale. Collectivist cultures have more rigid groups and have a more hierarchical societal system, organised according to factors such as age, sex and status, unlike the structure of individualistic cultures. Collectivists place emphasis on who the person is, whilst in individualistic cultures there is attention to what the person does. The contrast between the two cultures will be discussed by examining specific themes, such as societal roles, social groups, tight versus loose cultures, cognitive structures and emotional expressiveness.

Societal roles

The more complex and industrialised a society, the more individualistic the culture. This is because people have more specific roles in industrialised societies; in less industrialised societies their roles are more diffused and tend to overlap (Triandis 1987); for example, in a less industrialised society, the postman can also be the local shop delivery man and priest. There is more emphasis on the personality of the person, and no distinction is made between the ideas and the person who holds them. In western cultures, these are differentiated and people may relate to each other without intimacy and only for a specific reason, in a specific setting – for example, a postman or a repair man in England is only seen as such, whilst in a country like Cyprus there would be more value placed on the person as a whole and more personal details would be exchanged during a social interaction. In the more westernised type of society, the interest is only in what the person does and not in his or her political or religious stance.

Social groups

Social groups (such as the family or peers) can be inclusive or exclusive. Inclusive groups allow strangers to enter and leave the group freely whilst exclusive groups can be very mistrusting of anyone outside the group. Those in the exclusive groups tend to belong to the group for a long period, if not permanently. This is related to the fact that collectivist types of societies encourage physical proximity to relatives and friends; generally, there is less physical mobility in this group due to job changes, etc. This is evident in small communities in Ireland for example, whilst in big cities like London, there is more contact with different people and thus it is usual for neighbours or work colleagues to continually change. This creates more openness to other groups and there is generally more trust. Collectivist groups tend to have more insular social institutions, and outsiders are not fully accepted. In collective communities relationships are close-knit and there is little contact between groups. This leads to the belief that strangers are not to be trusted. If there are conflicts within the group, the members prefer to resolve them without outside help. It has usually been my experience with clients from Ireland for example, that they are less willing to undergo counselling than the Irish who have lived in England for a long time. Clients from America accept the idea of seeking psychological help more readily. Clients from Ireland view counselling as something one undergoes when there are grave problems, whilst for Americans, seeking help from a counsellor – rather than from the family – is part of the culture. In individualistic cultures, social groups are more detached and flexible, are usually chosen by individuals and can be changed any time. The members of individualistic cultures can often be intimate with several groups simultaneously and generally can have more flexibility in choosing relationships.

Tight versus loose cultures

Triandis (1990) makes a further distinction between 'tight' cultures and 'loose' cultures. Tight cultures are characterised by a rigid organisation, more homogeneity and general intolerance of uncertainty. For example, traditions and rituals may remain the same over time; this provides a predictable direction, along with specific expectations. There is more predictability, certainty and security. In loose cultures, there is more deviation from the norms and thus more heterogeneity.

Cognitive structures

The two types of cultures, collectivist and individualistic, also differ further in cognitive structures, although this is no substantial proof of actual biological differences (Triandis 1987).

For instance, one aspect of cognition is perceptual selectivity, what people choose to focus on. It is believed that cultural learning influences perceptual selectivity. In other words, cultural learning can have an impact on the values we hold; these lead us to place more importance on particular behaviours and less on others. For example, a father who beats his son is regarded differently in different cultures: for a collectivist culture, the father is the authority figure and is expected to exercise family control, so the action is seen to be justified. This can be witnessed in countries like Cyprus and Greece, where there is high value on the family background and status of the individual. In a more individualistic culture, such as Britain, the action is not seen to be justified, regardless of who committed the act. In collective cultures, public scrutiny and reputation are vital. If a member of a family has problems, the whole family's reputation may be at stake. This is most pronounced in Middle Eastern and Latin countries. This is quite a different notion than in western countries where there is more emphasis on individuality.

Emotional expressiveness

There are also variations in what is considered 'appropriate channelling' of emotions. In some cultures, Japan for instance, emotions must be controlled; in others, such as Southern European cultures, they are expressed more openly. Consequently, the Japanese are often labelled as 'cold' and Southern Europeans as 'over-emotional' by Northern European cultures. Differences in emotional expression were evident in a 'Cross-cultural psychology' course I taught, in the way the American students readily volunteered information about their personal or family patterns, whilst the South American, Middle Eastern, Japanese, Singaporean and Chinese students would only reply when asked specific questions and even then, they replied reluctantly. Americans place emphasis on the individual, emotional expression is encouraged as 'healthy' and the 'talking cure' is promoted. In comparison with other countries, the American family unit is less exclusive of outsiders and people tend to be more trusting of others, so family practices may be more readily shared with outsiders. For other cultures, personal information is protected and the family unit is more exclusive; there is preservation of self and family status; reputations become important and relevant to the whole family; strangers are not trusted; and certain topics are taboo areas.

The differences between collectivist and individualistic and tight and loose cultures may be evident, but we must be cautious not to create new generalisations and subsequently more stereotyped beliefs. This is because, as I have already pointed out, there are many differences even within one country; for example, in the South of Italy there is generally more collectivism than in the North. Another prominent example is the difference between the Scottish, Irish, Welsh and English subcultures. Finally, as stated earlier, culture is a flexible concept and even within a short period of time cultural ideas and patterns can change dramatically.

BODY GESTURES AND LANGUAGE

Variations in the language of gestures (such as facial expression and interpersonal distance) as well as verbal communication can create misunderstandings in cross-cultural communication. Understanding the meaning attached to these behaviours is dependent on the place and function they have within their culture of origin. Misunderstandings can often arise when the therapist attaches his or her own cultural explanation to particular behaviours or gestures. For example, each person has their own interpersonal distance, which is also dependent on cultural referents. There are cultures which encourage physical contact (for example, Mediterranean cultures) and others (such as East Asian cultures) who do not. In cultures which are very physical, people tend to have more eye contact and the interpersonal distance is shorter (Triandis 1990). In less physical cultures, eye contact may be seen as threatening or disrespectful. All aspects of body and verbal language should be considered in counselling work. For example, physical distance can create difficulties when the counsellor misunderstands the client's intention in sitting further away or in having very little eye contact. It is essential to allow the client to utilise the interpersonal distance that is comfortable and to use the desired eye contact and emotional expression that is authentic to the individual.

The words used in a certain language may have such a complex underlying meaning that only someone who shares a similar cultural background can fully comprehend the meaning of it. Each culture has its verbal localisms, specific cultural nuances of symbols, hidden meanings and subtle variations; a cultural understanding of nuances, imagery and special language cues and metaphor communication which may not be understood by outsiders. It has been suggested that some ethnic groups tend to use more associative, context-dependent information processing. In this case, the context of the language spoken may be of major importance to the conveyed meaning. A good example of this is the Japanese who do not often say 'no'; instead, they use many alternative words such as 'maybe' to convey the same meaning. To an English-speaking person this may seem an indirect way of communicating, but if the language is understood within the context of the Japanese culture it is much easier to grasp the intended meaning. When clients have to communicate in a language that is not their native language, important aspects of experience may be left out (Romero 1985). For example, some clients may intellectualise the problem and the emotions, rather than giving a direct, spontaneous response. This may also be due to the translation process, because the spontaneity of speech is lost.

STEREOTYPING/ETHNOCENTRICISM

Within any given culture, values and beliefs are usually accepted and reinforced by the members. This is extremely functional in that it creates common meaningful concepts, values and beliefs which form a shared basis for effective communication. However, cultures can also become somewhat closed systems where new information is not allowed to get through. Subsequently, they react to their own cultural patterns as 'natural' and 'correct' and anything that is different is rejected as 'incorrect' or is labelled 'strange behaviour'. Outsiders may be seen as threatening because they are perceived as inferior and as threatening the existing cultural identity, which upholds certain measures of normality.

Any deviation from the what one cultural group perceives as 'normal' gives rise to prejudices and stereotypes about those who belong to a different race or culture. We have preconceived ideas about people we have never even met, which undoubtedly influence our intergroup and interpersonal relationships. This can be demonstrated by a study run at an International College in London (Eleftheriadou and Hassanain 1986). Seventy-two college students, representing twenty-four different nationalities, were asked to attach specific adjectives to different cultures. The results showed that the most commonly attributed adjectives were friendly, open, loud and fun-loving/carefree for Americans, friendly, outgoing and loud for Greeks, friendly, hardworking and religious for Indians and aggressive, wealthy and loud for Arabs. Although the respondents had come into contact from people with other cultures and had friends among them, when they were asked to complete the survey they revealed certain common stereotypes.

Stereotypes, of race, gender, religion and social class amongst others, are important to consider in therapy, because through them we create rigid images of a whole culture and do not allow for individuality within a culture. Even when our view of an individual changes through one-to-one interaction, often the stereotype of his or her culture remains unchanged. This is because there is societal pressure to accept the stereotypes we create of other cultures. These become fixed in people's minds, and when new cultural practices are encountered it is extremely difficult, sometimes even impossible, to consider them as 'different but equal', since our own cultural beliefs and practices are constantly being reinforced as correct. There is a danger that stereotypes can be used to categorise cultures into inferior and superior positions in society. In order to consider an alternative way of thinking, many psychological adjustments have to be made. This is a dynamic process and it takes time. Many psychology experiments of perception illustrate how we become fixed in our cultural view of objects, people and situations. One such experiment that illustrates this clearly is the diagram shown below (see Figure 2). When people are asked to join the nine dots in the figure with four continuous lines they find it difficult.

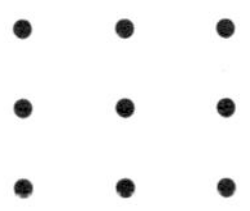

Figure 2

This is because they see the end of the dots as the end of the boundary of the problem. They do not therefore think to move beyond the boundary (as shown in Figure 3). In the same way we can become stuck in one way of thinking and unable to shift our perspective.

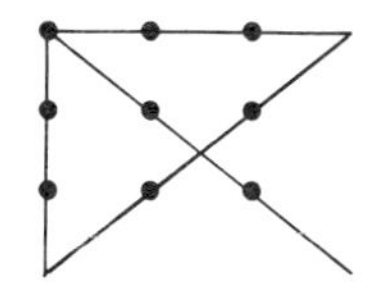

Figure 3

DISCUSSION ISSUES

1 Drawing from your own experience as (1) a client and (2) a therapist, do you think it is necessary that the counsellor and the client belong to the same racial/cultural background?

2 Think of an experience you have had in which you encountered cross-cultural barriers.

4

Transcultural Counselling in Practice

> To take what there is and use it – this is doubtless the right way to live.
>
> (Henry James)

In this section, the issues raised in the previous chapters will be integrated to provide a framework for working with clients from different cultures. The whole therapeutic process will be studied using the existential and phenomenological framework and some aspects of psychodynamic therapy. The process will be broken into artificial parts in order to highlight why and how each one is an essential ingredient. The starting point is a view of what the client and therapist bring into the therapy and what they expect to gain from it. Although both members contribute to the therapeutic relationship, the focus will be primarily on the skills the counsellor uses and his or her aims in using them. Most of the suggestions in the following sections are relevant to any psychotherapeutic communication, regardless of the approach used. However, as long as they are displayed in a consistent and convincing manner, they are particularly appropriate when working with clients from different cultural or ethnic backgrounds and those who bring cross-cultural conflicts.

MOVING FROM CROSS-CULTURAL TO TRANSCULTURAL COUNSELLING

The framework

The key word in the cross-cultural field is variation. We should recognise that every school of therapy has developed its own unique stance, belief systems, ethos and underlying philosophy from the culture or sub-culture in which it has arisen, and it may therefore not be applicable universally. At times, a particular approach may not even be applicable to those who belong to the same cultural background. This does not imply that, in practice, the counselling technique has to be changed completely to accommodate for each client. In fact, many practitioners would be critical of the very flexible counsellor. Nor does it mean that we have to apply different skills and focuses to suit a particular culture, because of the client's different descent or heritage. Rather, the inclusion of culture should be seen as an expansion of the existing counselling approaches. The aim should be to construct a more flexible way of working, where each client is seen as an individual. There has to be a way of organising and making sense of what the client presents, but it should be used as a framework and not a systematic, prescribed way of working. What is being suggested here is a model that is transcultural, rather than cross-cultural or intercultural. 'Cross-cultural' implies that we go across or 'inter' culture in trying to understand another person. That is, we use our own reference system to understand the client's experience rather than going beyond our own worldview. The difference between cross-cultural and transcultural is a crucial one because 'trans' denotes that counsellors need to work *beyond* their cultural differences. Here it is suggested that existential/phenomenological analysis can transcend culture, because it delves deep into the basic beliefs and values of the client, as defined by the client, and examines the client's fundamental ideas and assumptions about human existence within his or her construction of the world. It takes the view that both participants in the counselling process hold unique worldviews (see Chapter 1).

The counsellor's role: facilitator or expert?

The first step in transcultural counselling is for therapists to examine their own psychological processes and their relationship to their culture. This awareness includes a close examination of familial and interpersonal relationships and values, religious or political ideas, stereotypes, prejudices and racism, in order to clarify generally ideas on living. A therapist's worldview will inevitably play a major part in the therapy scenario. As Cohn states: 'most therapists . . . whatever technique they use . . . can never eliminate themselves – their view and feeling – from the total therapeutic situation' (1966: 4). Consequently, it is more important for therapists to be aware of their underlying personal philosophy and subsequent approach to counselling than to claim that they are practising in an indirective way. This is necessary because issues of *cultural distance* (Furnham and Bochner 1986) may interfere in the counsellor–client relationship. Cultural distance refers to the gap between cultures, which is generated by differences in abstract as well as concrete aspects. A counsellor and client who share a common culture are likely to be less culturally distant than two people from different cultures. Additionally, other practical issues such as whether the counsellor's own cultural or racial background affects his or her attitude towards the client must be examined.

It has been shown repeatedly that the counsellor's value systems can, and often do, influence the therapeutic work with the client (Khan 1991). The therapist must be careful not to create a sense of sameness with the client merely because he or she is trying to be an understanding therapist. On the contrary, this can be a response of a therapist who cannot separate himself or herself from the client. If there is too much identification with the client the therapist is not allowing the client to express his or her own powerful feelings. The client can experience this as unhelpful and restrictive. Whatever the intentions of the therapist (and these must be examined) the clients must be left to fight their own battles, as this is a part of the healing process. This does not mean that the therapist is a uninvolved bystander; it implies the therapist facilitates what the client wishes to discuss rather than thinking or feeling on behalf of the client.

Other important issues are whether the counsellor can acknowledge, understand and accept the client's cultural background, and whether his or her expectations about the client's culture will affect the speed and outcome of the therapy. The counsellor should learn about his or her clients' cultures, but this learning should be done with caution and openness to avoid stereotypes. When outsiders have some knowledge about other cultures, perhaps based on a book or a documentary, there is a danger that they will stereotype clients, believing that they are likely to present certain issues. It is not expected that the transcultural counsellor should learn about every culture, but it is important for him or her to become aware of the range and variety of values, beliefs and behaviours. Acknowledging that he or she is not fully informed about a culture may show an honesty that is appreciated by the client and is reciprocated by an explanatory account of his or her cultural practices. Becoming aware of diverse practices means that there is an attempt to see the client in terms of his or her own reference system rather than the counsellor's. The client's unique interpretation of the world is at all times embedded in his or her culture and this must be recognised by the therapist. When cross-cultural clients present symptoms which fit into western psychiatric categories, it is common for western mental health professionals to label them as having a psychiatric condition. The explanations given for clients' behaviours are often derived from the western culture. This may not be helpful. For example, informing a non-western client who is illiterate that his or her public speaking phobia is related to the problem of failure will be misunderstood, because it is a totally alien and irrelevant way of thinking for the client. Instead of dismissing the person as crazy or too culturally distant to work with, because his or her ideas are defined according to a different reference point, the counsellor works with feelings and behaviours and also examines the client's basic value system. It is important to remember that the client will eventually give the counsellor all the information that is necessary and relevant for the counselling sessions.

Therapy is a potential learning environment not only for the client, but also for the therapist. The self-exploration process, especially in acknowledging racism and prejudices, is life-long, and one never reaches a stage of full self-awareness. If the therapist has acknowledged these issues then he or she is able to discuss the client's concerns openly without allowing his or her own cultural issues to contaminate the client's. In addition, regular discussion and supervision of the therapeutic work with other professionals can be of great benefit, however experienced the counsellor may be.

THE THERAPEUTIC RELATIONSHIP

The therapeutic relationship between a counsellor and a client is unique because it is a relationship between those two particular people, with a certain social context, at a certain point in time. The two participants in this process are engaged in finding a meeting point where clear communication and understanding can take place. In any interaction, participants must have common referents and these are usually agreed through communicating about exactly what is being understood. Even if the counsellor and client are extremely culturally distant, existential/phenomenological analysis uses the material the client brings to the therapy to go deep into the values, morals, assumptions and expectations that people have about themselves and others. By exploring these the counsellor tries to gain insight into the culture as a whole, in order to discover what is considered appropriate individual behaviour. The therapeutic relationship will be illustrated through the use of the *emic* and *etic* distinction (after the linguistic words phonetic, meaning universal vocal utterances and phonemic, meaning sounds which are culturally unique).

An emic viewpoint is when a person or a group looks at cultural practices from within that culture. They can only view them through a subjective lens, as they are members of that culture and are familiar with it. But a person like a European mental health professional looking into African culture has an outside or etic view. He or she is not a member of that culture and will view it differently. In the same way, both the counsellor's and client's views are relevant, but they serve different purposes. The counsellor should never lose sight of his or her own ideas during the therapy; however close the communication he or she cannot experience exactly what the client is feeling. The priority is always to focus on the client, but at the same time to be aware of the feelings stirred in the therapist. This is a very difficult state for the therapist to reach and will be discussed in more detail below.

The counselling relationship should be as equal as possible; this may be achieved by focusing on the 'relationship'. The counsellor is *with* the client, alongside him or her, rather than being the professional person or expert on the client's life. A positive and supportive relationship needs to be developed. It requires time for the client to trust the counsellor in order to develop the *therapeutic alliance*. The therapeutic alliance means that both therapist and the client trust each other and their counselling relationship, and that the credibility (see pp. 41–6) ascribed to the counsellor is such that the client is able to work with him or her. A client enters therapy with the intention and the motivation to work through conflicts or find out more about himself or herself. It is also a time of admitting that assistance is needed to deal with a problem in life. The commitment to go through this process, share it with someone and take responsibility for it has to be internally accepted, otherwise the work cannot progress. When these elements have been established, then the problem(s) begin to be revealed, identified and described. Therapy is a two-way process and if the therapeutic alliance is not established, then this should be explored by looking at the two people's interrelationships. In transcultural counselling this may include an exploration of the feeling towards a racially or culturally different counsellor. The counsellor must be ready to accept and listen to the client, even if he or she expresses anger or general mistrust towards the majority culture. If the therapist can listen and be open to those feelings from the beginning it is a way of progressing and building up trust in the process.

The first session: setting the therapeutic culture

In all societies, the therapeutic situation is characterised by certain rituals that are culturally determined and should be understood by the service users (Torrey 1972). For example, industrialised societies tend to have a more clearly defined therapeutic system; time is very important, the therapeutic sessions are kept to a rigid schedule and the setting is kept as consistent as possible. This is unlike psychiatric consultations in Indian villages, where there is more flexibility in terms of time, the setting may not always be the same and it is common to find spiritual healers or even psychiatrists working in public places.

It is therefore necessary in the first counselling session to make the therapeutic culture explicit to the client. The first session may determine whether the client will return for further counselling sessions. There is a danger that if the client has not been *acculturated* (or integrated, to a certain degree, into the new societal culture) right from the onset of therapy (from the moment the client walks into the therapy room), he or she will leave the therapy. Cultural judgements based on the counsellor's own cultural reference system are easily made. For example, in the American Indian culture, one of the ways to show respect is not to engage in eye contact. If the counsellor is a non-American Indian therapist, he or she may interpret this as shyness, withdrawal or poor self-esteem. If the client is greeted in an inappropriate way and asked questions which he or she thinks are obtrusive, the trust and rapport cannot build up. It does not imply that difficult or taboo areas for the client should never be discussed, but that depending on the cultural background they may take longer to approach.

Clients will have their own beliefs, experiences, attitudes and expectations about setting and techniques, the therapist's role and therapeutic manner and their role as client as well as their own perception of the therapeutic process and its goals. If the client has never been to counselling, it is important to establish what ideas, goals and expectations he or she may have of therapy. The therapist can clarify the process to the client by contributing to his or her ideas and expectations. It is desirable that the 'therapeutic culture' which the client and counsellor will be working within be understood and accepted by the client; this is often not the case as information is not made explicit by the therapist. In the first session, psychological and physical boundaries are set (for example, distance between the chairs), as well as forms of address (for example, whether a handshake is appropriate, the name the person prefers to be addressed by) and non-verbal communication (such as silence, facial expressions, eye contact, interpersonal distance, body orientation). In the initial meeting the therapist should also include a brief account of how he or she works, with details of the timing of the session, the frequency of the sessions, whether the therapy is short or long-term, the fee and payment methods for the sessions and any other practical matters.

The therapist should also establish, directly or indirectly, whether he or she and the client are able to relate to each other. Somehow the counsellor has to get an idea of what the client's concerns are, and what his or her goals are for therapy. This is not like a formal medical assessment, but something which takes place throughout the therapy together with the client. Many clients will try to avoid taking responsibility for their own expectations and shift it instead onto the therapist, asking 'What shall I do?' The therapist explores these questions with the client; usually the client will have some idea of which direction they should take.

Therapeutic goals

One of the aims of transcultural counselling is that there should be some negotiation between the counsellor's model of the world and the client's. This may mean that the counsellor needs to be much more explicit than usual about his or her own philosophy and therapeutic approach and should try to communicate it in a way that is meaningful to the client. This is where the emic and etic models come into play and the bridging between the two is in its elementary stages. This is a difficult process and if the therapist does not meet the client's views with openness, misinterpretations are likely to occur. The counsellor's role in transcultural counselling is to promote the client's natural coping mechanisms rather than imposing something that the therapist believes in, or worse, imposing something foreign.

The focus of the therapy should be what the client has brought to the counselling, without an imposition of solutions from the therapist (Rogers 1951). The client is seen as an autonomous person who can only change if he or she is motivated and has chosen to do so. Therapists must always begin at the client's starting point or level, in terms of his or her worldview and problems and conflicts. The aim should be to provide the client with the opportunity to clarify, question and subsequently expand his or her worldview. People can end up in the situation where they have lost responsibility for themself and for their world. Many people who enter into the counselling process have reached this point in their life, when their choice and freedom seem extremely restricted. If we take the time to explore the direction in which our life is going, then we can accept ourselves and our situation, take responsibility for our own life and therefore gain the freedom to choose whether we want to change. Clients can try to see themselves more realistically and clearly, from a different perspective, along with new possibilities. At times, seeing a distressing situation in a new perspective can provide hope and motivation for the client and simultaneously facilitate emotional release. This appears as a gift for the client because therapy appears to be 'working'. It is not that the actual problem must be seen as something that necessarily has to be changed, but instead can seen as something that can be understood in a creative way. Therefore, the ultimate goal for clients is for them to have a better understanding of their feelings and behaviours, which is interlinked with creating their own unique interpretation of their experiences and feelings. Psychological exploration is something which must be experienced and understood on an emotional level by the person. It is by no means solely an intellectual process. Clients who have never engaged in an inward exploration of themselves and their relationships may find this difficult and resist the process, but when they come to a crisis they usually experience a motivating force to move from the old patterns (however secure they seemed to have been in the past). For many people, a crisis can indicate how little inwardly equipped they are to cope with life. Therapeutic involvement cannot rid them of the crisis, but they can learn to use their inner resources to cope with it and learn to become better equipped for the inevitable crises of life. In other words the counsellor has to help the client change old, unhelpful ways of thinking and behaving to more adaptive patterns. Often having a counsellor who is open enough, adequately trained and most importantly, psychologically strong enough to stay with their intense feelings will make the confrontation of old beliefs and painful experiences seem manageable.

Striving for 'selfhood' and eventually wholeness is not achieved through rejecting culture. There is a place for all aspects of culture. However, problems arise if clients view culture as a rigid systematic and restrictive way of planning their life; they are then not accepting responsibility for their own life. They are merely accepting culturally imposed ideas without exercising any freedom of choice. This is because the images people are exposed to (through the media or other means) have been taken on board as being reality and the truth, rather than as mere representation that can be transformed.

Culture is a vast and complex system that has to be broken down in a manageable way during the therapeutic process. The client's value systems are therefore explored within four modes of relating, as described earlier, in order to unfold the total existence of the person, both the individual and cultural aspects (Vontress 1987). With the therapist as the facilitator, the client is helped to examine and question the four dimensions, the Uberwelt, Umwelt, Eigenwelt and the Mitwelt; some aspects of these are owned and others are rejected or altered. It is not as important to find the roots of these social patterns as to explore how the person has interpreted events and what is meaningful in his or her life. Subsequently, a flexible counselling framework is used; it is a 'map of human living, rather than a detailed description of how to tackle specific personal issues' (Deurzen-Smith 1988: 7). This is almost a mental checklist to ensure that the whole of the client's experience is explored. Through this broad framework, the client's life can be placed in some type of perspective, which in turn may enable the client to develop a new understanding in his or her life. In this way existential/phenomenological analysis contends that too much emphasis on technique and therapeutic exercises can impede actual understanding of the client. Instead what is emphasised is for therapists to be deeply involved, or 'be with' clients through their exploration of life issues and to be open enough to deal with whatever experiences and feelings will come up, rather than to detach themselves and suggest ways (for example, therapeutic exercises) in which clients can deal with life issues.

TRANSCULTURAL CARING

In order to engage in transcultural counselling we must examine the basic ingredient of counselling, the concept of care. The client's goals in counselling will be to reach a psychological state which the client perceives as 'normal', which will be dependent on personal, interpersonal and cultural factors. Since the counsellor and the client may be part of different cultural contexts we must examine the counsellor's notion of care. Care is the most basic form of considering or feeling for another human being and its components include empathy, concern, presence, trust and support. It is 'the essential component of human growth, development, well being' (Leininger 1987: 110). The ability to provide and accept care is essential for human survival. It is a way of helping people to adapt to the struggles of life by providing them with emotional and behavioural support and encouragement. It is culturally defined, according to particular beliefs, values and practices; in examining care in the cross-cultural context we use the term *transcultural caring* (Leininger 1987). Transcultural caring means that the counsellor must use the client's notion of care as defined by the client's culture or what is known as *cultural-care* rather than depend on his or her own notion of care. Cultural-care must be used in a creative way to allow the client to resolve his or her conflict and fulfil his or her needs. There are three principles to the theory of transcultural caring. First of all, the notion of *cultural-care preservation* is utilised in counselling. In other words, each culture defines the concept of care differently and the counsellor must respect and ultimately work within that system. Leininger (1987), for example, has been involved in studies to discover native thoughts and ideas. He has found specific *cultural-care constructs* for the Vietnamese culture, Mexican-Americans, Anglo-Americans and thirty-two other nations. For example, Anglo-American Caucasians were found to define a caring person as a person who alleviates stress, discomfort and anxiety. Another important element was to be provided with information about health and to be taught to be self-sufficient. In contrast, family sharing was considered as the most important care concept for the Vietnamese in the United States and harmonious relationships with others, especially family members, was the most important for Philippine Americans.

Secondly, the counsellor has to accommodate to the particular culture's practices, rather than expecting the client to accommodate to the counsellor's practices. This is termed *cultural-care accommodation*. For example, if a particular culture is hierarchical in terms of status (in this case professional versus layman), then the client may feel very anxious if he or she experiences equality in the therapeutic relationship. This is common with Japanese clients who find the equality of the therapeutic relationship very different to their normal ways of relating to professionals. In this instance, it does not imply that the counsellor should become directive towards the client, but the 'equality' way of relating must be acknowledged, as well as how difficult it is for the client to adjust to. The therapist, however, should have respect for the role of authority figures (for example elders) in the client's culture.

The third component of the concept of caring is *cultural-care repatterning*, which involves taking the client's and counsellor's care constructs and trying to integrate them in an explicit manner during the therapeutic process. Cultural-care repatterning is a process that takes place throughout therapy.

These concepts are important because they can usually link with clients' presenting problems and subsequently the goals set during therapy. Just as the client is asked to be explicit about his or her worldview and culture, so must the counsellor be explicit about the culture of the therapy and its 'rules'. The client then has enough information to make a choice about whether they need to work with a different therapist. We, as therapists have to recognise that at times our construct of care may be too culturally different to that of the client and that it may thus be more suitable to refer the client to someone who shares a similar construct.

CREDIBILITY

Cultural knowledge and culture-consistent goals in counselling must be linked to the concept of *credibility*. Credibility refers to the client's perception of the therapist as an effective and helpful person. There are two types of credibility, *ascribed* and *achieved*.

Ascribed credibility

Ascribed credibility refers to characteristics that a person is born with, such as age, sex and race. In some countries these characteristics result in more trust and respect. For example, in Southern European and Arab cultures there is generally more respect for and subordination towards the elderly.

The application of western forms of therapy to other countries or to culturally different groups is likely to be meaningless unless methods are adapted to fit the needs of the specific cultural group. In some countries, the way of 'adapting' the alien method has been to integrate western psychological techniques with local therapy, because the local way of behaving, or the local healers, may be the most respected. For example, the psychiatrist Sushrut Jadhav (Nafsiyat Workshop, 1992) has found that Asians have a preference for professionals who present themselves as experts, are more directive and provide more structure and guidance, because this is culturally familiar and acceptable. Indeed, some clients may drop out of the therapy when it is made explicit that the responsibility to stay in therapy is placed on them. For example, the client who is asked what he or she perceives as the problem may see the professional as being inadequate and leave the therapy. According to their expectations the professional's role is to be directive and give them advice on how to deal with their problem. Western ways of working such as meeting the client in the therapist's setting have to be questioned. With some cultural groups the therapist may have to develop credibility by relating to the client in a different way, for example face to face rather than a purely psychoanalytic way of the therapist sitting behind the client's couch; or the therapist may have to consider the possibility of visiting the client at his or her home. The therapist should be open enough to explore alternate ways in which he or she can develop rapport with clients who are unfamiliar to counselling.

Some professionals suggest that credibility can be gained by counsellors being of the same ethnicity as the client. A counsellor from the same ethnic background may help the client because (to an extent), there is a shared reality. When client and therapist share the same values, attitudes, norms, patterns of communication and language they are both in the same socio-cultural context. In this relationship the therapist's credibility may be established very quickly, and this has important consequences for the therapeutic process. There may also be negative effects when the client and counsellor are matched, such as the counsellor assuming that the client will think and act in the same way as him or herself. This is common when any two people meet and it can lead to misunderstandings, frustration and lack of rapport.

Draguns (1990) found that ethnicity was an important factor

generally for African, Hispanic, East Asian and Arab clients. Levine and Campbell (1972) have found that the more the client can identify with the therapist's ethnicity and background, the more they are able to work together. For example, a therapist of the same ethnicity may understand that for a client to alter his or her value system may mean becoming ostracised from their particular family, from friends or from that culture as a whole. Clients who hold strong religious beliefs may find it difficult or threatening to be counselled by someone who holds opposing views; for example, Orthodox Jewish clients or Evangelical Protestants may benefit most from a counsellor who shares their religious beliefs. Nonetheless, research findings have shown that although clients did prefer same race or ethnicity counsellors, therapeutic style was generally a more important factor than race. There is also research to show that some people purposely choose to go to a different ethnicity counsellor. Certainly in my own experience of therapy, I felt it was important to choose a therapist who understood about my cultural background, but because I feel part of both the Cypriot and English cultures, seeing an English counsellor did not create problems. In my clinical practice, it is interesting that the few Greek clients I have had have spoken to me in English. They prefer to converse in English because it creates enough distance for exploration, although because they know I am Greek they feel there is a shared cultural understanding. This is very important to bear in mind because a client may not want to work solely within their culture; they may want to find other creative resolutions which consider aspects of a new culture. The therapist of the same culture can often be 'stuck' in their own culture so much that they may feel threatened by the client's rejection of it. As a result they may try to enclose the client in a culture that is not appropriate for that client. If a therapist of a different culture is open-minded and has trained in the cross-cultural field then the process of exploration can work effectively. A therapist who is not part of the in-group may sometimes reinforce a further sense of confidentiality. A client may also choose a counsellor from the host culture because the client can identify with the host culture more than with his or her own cultural background. Another client may associate the white therapist with the police, the Home Office and other figures of authority that he or she feels anxious about. This may be because they have a certain power that the client cannot have in the host country. These issues must be considered by the therapist, together with the client.

Cultural patterns will undoubtedly influence the therapist and client relationship. This relationship tends to be more equal in a democratic socio-political system, whilst in an authoritarian system (where respect for authority figures or elders is emphasised) the counsellor may take on a more assertive and instructive role. Nonetheless, it does not mean that cultural incongruities (such as language, role confusion, different interpretations of behaviour, etc.) should always be bridged; for example, the therapist adapting cultural body gestures or language expressions to the client. In fact, 'cultural incongruities are often unavoidable and at times are necessary' (Sue and Zane 1987: 44). Matching a client and therapist ethnically, or indeed in any other way (for example, in terms of socio-economic status, age, sex, etc.), does not in any way ensure therapeutic success. Additionally, the research into client preference reflects the fact that many factors are intertwined in choosing how and where to seek help.

Achieved credibility

The second aspect of credibility is called achieved credibility. Achieved credibility has to do with the therapist's knowledge and skills. The client develops trust or confidence in the therapist as a direct reflection of his or her skills. So even if the client has had negative associations with the majority culture in the past, the skilled therapist can still demonstrate an ability for accurate listening and not reinforce the client's perception of the majority culture.

Achieving credibility involves utilisation of the basic counselling skills and the ability to assess the counselling interaction accurately, as well as showing cultural sensitivity. This is likely to make the client hopeful about dealing with his or her problems. For instance, a male client may have difficulty going to female therapists for cultural reasons, but may nevertheless learn from the experience, depending on the therapist's way of handling his problems. For example, in Arab cultures, males and older people hold the highest status, and in their perception, women have low ascribed credibility. Arab males may therefore believe that they cannot be helped by a female counsellor.

There are aspects of achieved credibility which apply not only to ethnic minority clients (even those who have been acculturated), but to any client. The first element is the conceptualisation or *naming* of the problem. Here, naming does not refer to naming a specific disease or problem according to psychiatric categories, but to a process which has resulted form the ongoing communication between the therapist and the client. It is a phenomenological description of what the client is going through. The counsellor tries to demonstrate to the client, through accurate reflection of the client's experience, an understanding of the client's experience. When the client is going through a situation of confusion alone, it can be extremely unsettling because the state of confusion is nameless. The sharing of feelings of itself can sometimes alleviate the sense of isolation. If the therapist makes links to the client's problems and situations which are incongruent with his or her experience it can result in loss of credibility. For example, the therapist may ask the client to take part in an exercise where they have to confront their parents about something. To the therapist this communication may be a way forward, but to the client the act itself my be unacceptable, as well as the suggested content possibly alienating him or her from the parents. Even if the therapist has an idea of what is at the root of the problem it is extremely dangerous to communicate it to the client when he or she is not ready, and could cost the loss of the client from therapy. This is the reason why there should not be any suggestion from the therapist about what the client should think, say or act.

Another element of achieved credibility is what has been called the *Principle of Rumpelstiltskin* (Torrey 1972). This name comes from the Brothers Grimm fairy tales where the right words had to be said to create the desired effect. This refers to the client's ability to identify the event (or series of events) that directly or indirectly have created unwanted emotions and behaviours. At the same time, the naming can bring out associated connections to other events, which were previously excluded from consciousness. For example, a client may realise that certain current behaviour is linked to a traumatic incident in childhood. At the time of the incident the behaviour may have been a way of coping with painful emotions, but in later life it proves restricting. The association to an earlier event usually results in connections to other events where the client has used the same behaviour or expected other people to behave in a particular way. These connections may result in confusion, followed by an acknowledgement of the emotions experienced and their significance to the client. The nature of the problem may change after the initial stages of therapy, and become more refined as the therapeutic process progresses, when new information slowly becomes incorporated. But the problem must at all times be perceived in a way that is congruent with the client's belief systems, otherwise the credibility of the therapist may be lost. Identification of the essential agents of the problem proves to the client that he or she is being understood by the therapist.

A third aspect of achieved credibility concerns the goals of therapy. The therapist's skills may be tested in a cross-cultural situation, where the client and therapist may have different goals. This is because often, in my experience, therapists try to bring the client to their way of thinking rather than accepting the client's goals as being valid.

Generally, however, credibility cannot be established solely by knowing the cultural background of the client. Instead, each individual case must be looked at as being unique, as well as truly experienced through the therapeutic relationship.

GIVING

If the counsellor is listening accurately, the individual needs and concerns of the client will begin to be met. This links with the second essential component of therapy, which is the process of *giving* (Sue and Zane 1987). This refers to any meaningful gain the client obtains from therapy. It is useful, especially in the early sessions, when the therapist's credibility is likely to be tested. Types of gifts or rewards for the client include accurate reflection of his or her experience, reduction or total alleviation from negative symptoms, behaviours or emotions, empathic understanding, catharsis, clarity in thought processes, skill acquisition or skill recognition. As a result of the 'giving', the client's coping mechanisms are activated, goals are set, reassurance is obtained and hope and faith are invested in the counselling process and/or in themselves. The process of giving is necessary, because clients have a greater tendency to drop out of therapy in the earlier stages. It is a way of gaining the client's trust and motivation by demonstrating a different perspective to a problem. For the client, this does not mean reaching solutions, but implies changes in self-perception or interrelationships, or simply a change in attitudes.

TRANSFERENCE AND COUNTERTRANSFERENCE

Powerful emotions are stirred in all of us when we are relating to others, especially with those we are closely involved with. We experience feelings and invoke feelings in other people as a result of our own interpersonal experiences and how we have interpreted them. In psychoanalytic therapy, *transference* refers to the client's old childhood patterns and behaviours toward significant others which are repeated in the therapy scenario by being transferred on to the therapist. *Countertransference* refers to the feelings experienced by the therapist which are evoked by the client. However transference and countertransference are a result of both intrapsychic processes and interrelationships and they do not run purely from the client to the therapist. It is a much more complicated process, in which the therapist plays an equally important part to that of the client. The therapist will arouse certain feelings and experiences in the client which the client will relate to his or her own experiences. Therefore in the transference for example, the client may project onto the therapist something that was triggered off in him or her by the therapist's way of dress, body or facial expression, or verbalisations. Similarly the countertransference, or feelings experienced by the therapist during the therapeutic encounter, is a result both of the client's experiences and of something which has touched the therapist's feeling. Although counsellors are required to undergo a great deal of personal development during training it does not imply that they can eventually become 'objective' or do not have strong reactions to the clients. This is a view of two people interrelating, rather than an expert who does not have emotions and a client who does. It is not an easy process to allow oneself to feel during the therapy, but doing so can actually be very healing for the client because it communicates to him or her that however painful the emotions will be there is someone listening and able to bear them. In therapy the transference and countertransference are intensified because it is an environment which is set up to focus on powerful emotional experiences. For example a person who experienced a great deal of emotional abuse during childhood may be mistrustful of other people and expect others to treat them in a similar way. What the client brings into the therapy room is usually something that has been experienced in reality and has been translated internally and, at times, the feelings of the original experience are projected onto other people. Transference and countertransference do not occur only in the therapy room, but exist outside it. Clients hold fantasies and ideas about the therapist even before they meet, based on previous experiences and even historically transmitted ideas of race and culture. In every relationship, there is some level of transference towards other people, whether it is negative or positive. Transference and countertransference occur whether the counsellor and the client share the same racial or ethnic background or not.

The usefulness of transference and countertransference as therapeutic tools in cross-cultural counselling is controversial. Here, both of these concepts are seen as useful if they are used in accordance to cultural beliefs and practices. Transference and countertransference, as defined above, imply that both participants in the counselling process are active, and they both have their own feelings about the other person, so they are very useful counselling tools. This implies that they can be used even with clients who do not have a good grasp of the English language, to explore the client's feelings, the therapeutic relationship and generally how the client relates to others. In this way an emotional understanding of the client's experiences can still take place.

Racism in the transference and countertransference

In transcultural counselling, one area that often brings about many powerful feelings and can lead to a breakdown of the relationship is racism. Racism, like sexism, may be subtle, but it is always present on some level in all of us. For example, for a black client and a white therapist there may be feelings of one being inferior to the other. Because they have been brought up with the confidence of their superior position, a white person may feel that anything other than 'whiteness' is inferior. Alternatively, if a black client has encountered racism in the past he or she may expect anyone who is white to exhibit racist attitudes. The effect of this on the therapist's worldview and subsequently the effect on the counselling relationship must be explored. When a black client works with a black therapist the feelings of countertransference can be very powerful. If a black client has strong feelings of self-hate it can evoke a strong countertransference for a black therapist, who may be reminded of his or her own difficulties or pain. Another way of dealing with racism is to be extremely mistrustful of the therapist as someone who cannot be helpful to a black person. The client in this case may be extremely angry because of his or her previous mistreatment from white people and may resist any communication from the therapist.

Who then should bring up the issue of race in the therapy room, the client or the therapist? In this book, it is suggested that it should be the therapist and not the client. If the therapist does not pick up cues (which is often the case), there is the danger that clients may be too afraid to bring it up or that they may be too caught up with their own difficulties to be in touch with the negative transference, let alone to express it. This is a delicate issue because the client may fear that if negative feelings are introduced he or she cannot develop a good working relationship with the therapist. These negative feelings can be very powerful and seem persecuting for the therapist. It is essential therefore for the therapist to have carried out his or her own self-development, in order not to feel attacked by the negative feelings and to be able to bear them. In other words the therapist needs to be aware of his or her countertransference feelings in the therapy, in order to separate the feelings of the client from those of the therapist so that they do not impose on the client. It is also crucial that the issue of race is brought up at the correct time, otherwise a premature reflection of the client's feelings can be frightening and appear accusatory. Cues are taken at all times from the client's communications.

EPOCHE, RULES OF DESCRIPTION AND HORIZONTALISATION

The counselling process consists of several elements – *epoché, the rules of description and horizontalisation* – that should occur simultaneously. First, it is important to discuss epoché in terms of the concepts of sympathy and empathy. Sympathy is the recognition that both the client and the therapist experience similar human emotions. Empathy is the process whereby the counsellor listens to and tries to understand the client's subjective worldview. It is the ability to 'enter the client's internal experience of the world as far as possible in order to reflect it back as accurately as [the counsellor is] able' (Spinelli 1989: 130), along with the recognition that this can be achieved only to an extent and only after a period of time of working with the client. It requires the building and strengthening of bridges between the 'emic' and 'etic' constructions of the world (as described above), so as to allow clearer and more specific material to be expressed. The first prerequisite of therapy is to be as bias-free as possible, through finding a middle way between using pure theory and total personal involvement. The former would not benefit the client, because it is far too impersonal and it would not allow an authentic human relationship to develop. The latter would be too invasive for the client and thus not helpful, because the therapist can become so involved with the problem that he or she experiences it as his or her own. We aim rather for an inbetween state, called epoché. It is a process of stepping back from as many of our usual assumptions or prejudices as possible in order to understand the client's world, but without entering it. We cannot rid ourselves completely of prejudices or biases, but even the fact that they have been recognised can be helpful. It is like depositing them on a shelf for a while, rather than disowning them. Despite our necessary involvement in the counselling process, we also try to retain some objectivity or detachment. That way, there is not only respect for the clients but space for them to explore their own thoughts and feelings. The immediate focus is on experience as it happens, not on theory, belief or reason. The therapist attempts to be open to the client's worldview, without losing touch with his or her own racial, ethnic and cultural background. Because we can never be sure what is 'culture-free' in the counselling setting, it is important that we are open and flexible, continually checking and clarifying with the client, who is therefore allowed to be, accepted for what he or she is. This is equivalent to what Rogers calls *unconditional positive regard* or *unconditional acceptance*. It implies that we strive to be non-judgemental and respect whatever the client's feelings may be (see Rogers 1951). The focus is on feelings rather than on the action a client has decided to take. However much we disagree with the client's behaviour, as human beings are able to feel concern and tune into another's psychological pain. We are always affected in some way by clients and it is precisely this involvement that creates the authenticity or genuineness of the therapist. It is a process of being there *with* the client. Another vital counsellor attribute is the toleration of ambiguity or the ability to bear the client's confusion in his or her feelings and experiences and not to rush the client to make sense of them (see Rogers 1951). If the counsellor can provide the client with these qualities the client may build up faith and hope in the actual therapeutic process.

After the essential state of epoché, the next element is called the *rule of description*. This is an attempt to describe immediate here-and-now stimuli rather than formulating more abstract notions of what the stimuli might be. Thus the immediate behaviour of the client would be examined, with a focus on what is actually being experienced, rather than how it was experienced in the past or how he or she would like to experience it in the future. This is because experience is at all times cumulative; even when clients describe an early state which was extremely traumatic, it has usually been contaminated with beliefs and feelings from later experiences. For example, clients may try to make sense of difficult experiences by concentrating on certain elements or adding new material. Another important aspect of the counselling process is the *horizontalisation rule* or *equalisation rule*. This is an attempt to avoid hierarchies in the description of behaviour. All phenomena are accepted as normal, as the person's subjective reality. No attempt is made to assign a different ranking or level of importance to any one subjective experience. For example, if the client talks about several different painful life events it is not up to the therapist to direct the client as to which one is the most important to explore at that moment in the therapy. It is absolutely essential that the counsellor shows neutrality to the client, avoiding any criticisms or judgements. After all, even if the behaviour appears totally irrational to the counsellor, it has the meaning and purpose the client has attributed to it.

ENDING THERAPY

The ending stage of therapy may be defined as the end of a fixed schedule of sessions, or the stage when the client feels he or she has gained enough insight into a conflict or concern. It does not refer to a curative process, but to an agreed ending of the therapeutic process with the fulfilment of certain goals. The therapist should work towards the set ending time gradually, something which is essential if the relationship has been long-standing. There may be times when the therapist will feel that the termination is premature. There would then be exploration of the reasons for termination, although the client is still given the responsibility to decide what he or she feels is right. This is important because at times clients become overdependent on their therapists, which can slow down the therapeutic process. For the ethnic minority client this may be particularly damaging because their feelings of inferiority or mistrust may become intensified if they are not allowed to progress in therapy.

Therapy, as stated earlier, is a process of self-observation, and ending is a product of finding out about oneself and learning to use the insight gained to make desired changes and to cope with future events. The aspects of oneself that one begins to encounter can be unravelled, in order to discover whether they are part of what the client wants to be. Clients are often unaware that they have been living their lives according to other people's expectations of them rather than following their own wishes. In doing this, the client can often come to recognise which aspects of life he or she has lost control of and find ways of regaining control. It is useful to evaluate together with the client where he or she is in relation to the goals set in the initial sessions. This may be done through a summary of the therapeutic process and the type of issues that the client has had to identify, confront and/or change. It often comes as a surprise to clients to realise how far they have progressed, even if more counselling work is needed. At all times, it must be left up to the client to decide whether to continue or terminate the therapy. It is therefore important to note that this 'ending stage' is not defined as a stage when all problems have been resolved. Instead, the process of self-exploration and discovery is seen as life-long. There are three reasons for this. First, by the time the individual comes to therapy, he or she has been conditioned for so long that this conditioning cannot be completely altered solely through the therapeutic process. It may indeed take a lifetime to reassess old ways of relating and patterns that the person wants to change. Secondly, new decisions and a change of direction will inevitably contain their own contradictions, and thirdly, along the way, the individual comes to recognise further limitations in life (Deurzen-Smith 1988). By the latter I mean that resolving a problem may sometimes mean that in order to gain certain things in life, other things may have to be given up. For example, a client may realise that an old friendship is no longer fulfilling and is causing a great deal of anguish, but letting go of it may be equally difficult to do, especially if it has been long-term. In ending, it is hoped that the client has reached a point where he or she is better equipped to deal with the problems of life.

CASE STUDIES

Mary

A young West Indian girl, Mary, came to counselling because she felt she needed to find clearer ways of expressing her feelings. She felt very confused about whether she was truly 'black' or 'white', and she wanted slowly to be able to leave her parents. She had been living in England for most of her life and she saw this as permanent, in contrast to her family who considered it temporary. She was hesitant about engaging in counselling because it was a culturally unacceptable way of dealing with personal problems according to the West Indian part of her, although the western part of her had some hope in it as potentially helpful. She felt she had conflicts to deal with, but that if she entered counselling it would be a betrayal of her family's value system. In this case, one of the family beliefs was that everything which goes on within the family is private and must not be shared with outsiders. Consequently, she found it almost impossible to discuss her family and show any negative feelings towards them during therapy. Instead, she would engage in indirect signs of anger and other forms of expression that did not result in any resolution of her problems, such as alcohol consumption. She felt these indirect expressions were 'messy ways of showing feelings'. It was in fact one of her objectives to find other ways of releasing intense emotions. She came from a culture where elders and authority figures, particularly parents, must be respected. They are seen as people who provide everything for their children until they are of an age to leave home (sometimes this may mean when they get married). She was still living with her parents and therefore had to abide by their rules. Someone like this client may take a long time to engage in the counselling process and the deviation from their family's values may create a great deal of conflict. What is important is not to read this situation from only one perspective. In this example, the western perspective would suggest that Mary had not yet separated or become independent from her parents. But in some cultures, however 'independent' the children are, they remain at home. It is seen as quite unnecessary for the offspring to be living elsewhere when they have not yet created their own family. In therapy, the client's reasons for seeking counselling must be explored first, without imposing an opinion on what the problem appears to be. Furthermore, if a client is not ready for any changes or a re-evaluation of life, it is not up to the counsellor to impose it.

Stella

Stella, a Greek client in her mid-twenties, sought counselling because she was experiencing problems in adjusting to the British culture. She always talked to me in English, although she knew that I understood Greek. The fact that I was Greek 'did not bother her at all'. In exploring this during the therapy, she said however that she would not have come to counselling had I not been from the same culture. She said that because of the commonality of our culture I was more than a counsellor to her, I was also a friend and a fellow Greek. It was taken for granted that I understood about 'the behaviour of us Greeks'. This notion of being similar gave her many expectations; for example, that I could help because I represented the all-good Greek culture; any non-Greek represented the bad majority culture. It is common for clients who experience cross-cultural difficulties to split off the majority culture as being all bad and identify with their own as being the perfect one. The reverse can also take place, as it did for Maria.

Maria

Maria, a client from a Greek-Cypriot background in her early twenties, came to counselling because she was feeling controlled by external pressures. She was born in England and considered herself integrated into the English culture. She had indeed adopted many of the values of the host English culture, and felt she had not adopted many aspects of the Greek-Cypriot culture. In Maria's case I was someone who at times represented the 'modern, advanced English culture' and at times the 'old, undesirable Greek culture'. The two cultures were in conflict, leaving her unsure where she belonged. She had been involved with an Asian man (also from a minority culture), and this created further conflicts. On the one hand she identified with him and on the other she would project all her angry feelings onto him. This is not to say that the issue of culture was the only cause for the problems in her relationship with this man, but it intensified matters.

As counselling progressed, more ties to the original, parental background emerged. She began to recognise this during the sessions and was very surprised. In her social world she had developed very close ties to her immediate family members. This had created a great deal of conflict, because she was expected to fulfil a prescribed family role, which she felt was too demanding. She did not think it considered her own needs. These role expectations are not unusual for close-knit families. Maria felt she had no control over her life and felt she had to gain it somehow. In trying to integrate herself into another culture, she had convinced herself that she had adopted many of its values and beliefs. The external conflict with her family was representative of her internal conflict of feeling trapped by values she thought did not belong to her, and which with time she came to recognise as deeply implanted. She had clearly made value judgements as to which culture was most 'advanced' and it came as a surprise to her when she realised how much of the parental culture she had adhered to. Without this realisation it would have been difficult for her to progress in therapy. It also meant there was much work ahead of her to deal with this cross-cultural conflict. It is only when there is an increase in self-awareness that we can begin to change the things we want to change and accept other aspects of ourselves. Deeper understanding can help the client understand the particular role he or she has taken on board, often without realising how the role was acquired. In this case, Maria had started to gain insight into her experiences and she was able to understand more clearly how many of her relationships, with English men in particular, were creating internal conflict.

Maria ended counselling when she began to realise what values she held and why she had been experiencing so many conflicts. Awareness of values and beliefs was a necessary starting point, enabling her to become clearer about her own worldview. It was also a way of gaining more responsibility for her life, and more control now that she was more self-aware. She used therapy as a catalyst for her own process of gaining self-awareness, as well as redefining old meanings and attitudes. Many clients leave the therapy process when the first 'shifts' in value systems or beliefs begin to take place. This was the case for Maria.

Ella

Ella, a client from the West Indies, sought counselling because she was experiencing anxiety when she entered a car. The anxiety became worse every time she attempted to take her driving test. At first, she had tried taking relaxation pills, but they had not helped. After she failed the driving test several times, her doctor referred her to the counselling centre where I saw her. She described her goal as wanting to be able to drive in a relaxed manner, and consequently to pass her driving test. As the sessions progressed, it emerged that anxiety was experienced in many areas of her life; it was a type of panic at facing life which sometimes seemed almost to be coming from an external source. It was experienced in the presence of different people (including myself), and it also arose amongst groups of people. It was essential for me to find out exactly what the experience was like *for her* and not to make assumptions about anxiety on the basis of previous definitions of and associations with anxiety. This was explored through gentle questioning and reflecting on what she meant and how she experienced anxiety. Together, through a dialogue, we began this process where she would slowly describe how it was to feel anxious and how it affected her during the experience, how the experience came about, how she knew she was feeling anxious and how it presented itself, how it built up and what was being experienced before this anxiety, what preceded it in terms of thoughts and feelings, the duration of the experience, what happened when it was over, how it affected her moods and feelings, the long-term effects and so forth.

All these questions were necessary to understand this client's unique experience of anxiety. The counsellor may have worked with someone who had a similar problem, but he or she has never worked with this individual client before. In fact, when hearing a presenting problem (as it is appears to be in the initial sessions), it is easy to formulate hypotheses as to nature of the problem and the cause for the concern. Yet this is dangerous to the client, because by making those assumptions we may actually hear only those experiences of the client that fit in with our theories. It is worth reminding ourselves of the emic–etic distinction and that, as therapists, we are located in an etic stance and cannot make assumptions about how the client's subjective world is structured. Even if there are some common elements, there are also unique components for each individual, such as his or her connection to certain situations, times or settings. The clarification process is for the client and also for the therapist to understand the experience of feeling anxious. Clarification is essential because we often say we understand another person, when in reality we are making assumptions based on our subjective experience of a similar situation as that experienced by the client.

As therapy progressed, Ella began to explain how her

experience of anxiety was of generally feeling restricted and controlled. She had found coming to England particularly difficult because of the extreme differences between the two cultures. She had her own set of values about how she should act as a black person, as a woman and as a mother (and an endless number of other roles). She believed children should be brought up by their mothers and spent as much time as she could with them. She had worked part-time when she first came to England, but later stopped work altogether so that she could be home when her children came home from school. She preferred to deal with the domestic and child-rearing role, with her husband taking care of all the responsibilities of jobs outside the house. She felt she could not express herself authentically and at times she was unsure of who she was. Sometimes in the sessions this restricted way of living was expressed in the way she sat and the way she had her coat buttoned up to the top, with her purse crossing over her chest. In terms of her Eigenwelt, or personal world, she felt trapped and rather isolated from life, even from herself. She found it too difficult to be intimate with people and would always view life from a distance, as if she was a bystander who watched without involvement. It was like a feeling of 'acting' her societal roles (of mother and wife) rather than being engaged in them. The 'acting script' had been written since she was a young girl and she was determined to fulfil it. However, she found that now that she had reached her late thirties it had become far too limiting. Her children would see a perfect family with members who were always affectionate, but she felt her part in the family was somehow not genuine. In her Mitwelt, or social world, she described how she did not feel independent. She depended on her friends to drive her places, on her husband to control all the accounts and finances at home. She was treated as a child who has only limited responsibility. Being a dependent child had been beneficial to her, but with time she had begun to resent it. She also knew that when she had tried to take hold of some degree of responsibility she had ended up feeling so 'paralysed' that she was not able to manage it. This was a result of her many years without responsibility, and had become a way of life. Her physical world or Umwelt was also experienced as restricted in comparison to her life 'back home', in the West Indies. There, life consisted of 'really' feeling the weather and generally being more in touch with nature. She had always loved to walk outdoors and feel the hot sun, look at the blue sky, pick fresh fruit, etc. Coming to England was experienced as a restriction of her physical body. She slowly began to feel she could not just walk everywhere because of the weather, and she hated the cold and the rain. She found it depressed her and made her stay indoors more. The distances in London were greater so she could no longer walk to places, but had to take buses and trains, and this too was experienced as a restriction. She felt as if things were now being imposed on her; for instance having to learn to drive in order to be able to go out and have some independence. The means of transport may seem like a detail and not actually relevant to the counselling process, but it served as a means of opening up her experience of having to adjust to a whole new way of life and environment. Had it not been explored, it would have meant a denial of a major aspect of her experience. The need for careful exploration is emphasised in transcultural work, because we have to consciously step out of our usual framework of the world and ask the client questions about culturally shared meanings we normally take for granted. The adjustment to a new country was particularly significant for Ella, because she had had expectations and fantasies as a child of what it was going to be like to finally join her mother in England. Like many West Indians who had to stay when their parents came to England to earn a living, she had lived away from her mother up to adolescence. In many ways, the reunion with her mother was a disappointment, just as the weather and many other aspects of the new culture had been. The difficulties of her lonely childhood without her mother, the new culture and what she had left behind, as well as her family life in England, had all left unresolved feelings. In a way, not being able to drive was symbolic of her wish to be taken care of and not to become independent and do things as an adult. She was still behaving like a young helpless child.

Ending therapy, for Ella, was reaching a point where she had regained some control over and independence in her life. During the therapeutic process, all of her modes of relating were explored, by considering them in the past, present and future. In terms of the original goal, passing her driving test, she succeeded without any medication from her doctor. There was panic once she had passed the test and all the feelings of inadequacy returned, but somehow she fought them. She actually came to sessions in her car, was able to take the children places and go out with friends, which were all symbols of her independence. She still had difficulties being intimate with people and therefore avoided exposing her inner feelings and thoughts. She realised that she had created a type of safety net around her, and that she was quick to block others out when she felt threatened. She set out to deal with this. Her first project was to communicate with her mother. She had blamed her mother for not providing her with the security she wanted during early childhood, but had never tried to engage with her mother because of her anger and mistrust. That she had been abandoned was a reality, but what is important is how she experienced it and what meanings she had attributed to the experience. She began to recognise that, to a certain degree, she had created her own role. She set herself certain ways to help her deal with the role she played in her family which she began to recognise as no longer beneficial. She discovered that she had to find comfort and security within herself. Though she recognised the importance of other people in her life, choice and the responsibility to change remained with her. Creatively, or in her Uberwelt, she found that there were certain things she really enjoyed doing. Eventually, her passion for dance emerged as a way of releasing physical frustration. She actually 'needed' to do this once in a while, to expel worries and conflicts completely. Indeed, she would become quite a different person when dancing, and she would go on dancing for hours. It was a very cathartic experience for her and slowly she came to appreciate its importance. She also loved being with children and writing stories. However, this had never been expressed as she felt too restricted to engage in these activities. When one part of the client's world becomes restricted, other parts too become restricted.

The therapy finished when she felt it was time to communicate with her family in a way that felt more real to her. She realised that by not being truthful to herself for so long she had also distanced herself from her family and this situation could not go on any longer. It was a risk for her to expose more of her true feelings, but she felt more trusting of her immediate family than ever before.

DISCUSSION ISSUES

1 Describe your own process of differentiating your cultural socialisation patterns from those of a culturally different client.

2 Can you think of other therapeutic qualities that might be effective in transcultural counselling work? Are these universal qualities or culture-specific?

5

The Clients

> Experience is not what happens to a man. It is what a man does with what happens to him.
>
> (Aldous Huxley)

In this chapter the type of clients who enter cross-cultural counselling and the types of problems they bring to counselling will be identified. This will include an examination of the experience of moving to another culture and the different ways in which people deal with the changes involved. This will be discussed with clinical case examples.

THE CLIENTS

Everyone who is engaged in transcultural counselling needs to learn some background information about the cultures they are going to be working with. Culture and the individual are in constant interaction (as discussed earlier), so we need to understand what elements of the culture are important to the client and something about the particular culture those elements are drawn from. It is a way of gaining a balanced perspective between the internal (individual) and external (socio-cultural) worlds. The reason that many of the existing counselling approaches have not been effective with clients from different racial/cultural backgrounds is usually because they have only taken into consideration the intrapsychic world of the person. The transcultural framework, using ideas from existential/phenomenological analysis and psychoanalysis, attempts to find a state between the internal and the external worlds.

Learning about other cultures is a useful way of being aware how much values and behaviours vary across nations. On a micro-level this could mean understanding the meaning of different facial expressions or the role of food in the client's culture; on a macro-level it could mean having some understanding of the socio-political situation of a country. We need to know a client's psychical or economic/political reasons for moving to another country, because there is undoubtedly a difference between the people who are temporarily living in a country and those who are permanent immigrants. Furthermore, there is a difference between those immigrants who left their country of origin because of poor economic conditions as opposed to those who left because of psycho-social factors. Here, there is a distinction between the two factors in that the former group have very little choice compared to the latter group. For example, a Jewish American client I was counselling had left the United States for a short period because she was so unhappy with the pressure from her family and cultural group. In order to distance herself psychologically from them she found it easier to be physically distant (see Eleftheriadou 1993). Being aware of psychological and socio-political factors enables us to have more insight into what factors may motivate people to integrate themselves into the new society or not to integrate themselves as the case may be. Even those who leave their country of origin out of choice and become permanent residents of a country may not *perceive* themselves as permanent residents. A good example is Cypriots who move to London. Most of them see themselves as temporary residents who 'will go back one day'. This is the wish of many of the immigrant groups.

For the purposes of this book the ethnic minority groups have been divided into separate categories: internal migrants, ethnic minorities, white ethnics and temporary residents, although there is overlap between them. However, the terms 'ethnic minorities' and 'white ethnics' may be misleading because both the white and non-white immigrant groups may have been residents in the new culture for a long period or may have just arrived. In other words, they may be first, second, fifth or more generations removed from their ancestral roots; we cannot assume that because they come from different cultural roots they are newcomers.

Internal migrants

This category refers to the internal migration within Britain from Scotland or Northern Ireland. Although there are many cultural similarities with the rest of Britain, the Scottish and Northern Irish groups are very proud to be different in many ways and have fought for years to retain this difference.

Ethnic minorities

The first group of clients who are likely to enter cross-cultural counselling are ethnic minority immigrants. They tend to share racial characteristics, historical heritage and language. In Britain, the term ethnic minorities refers mainly to non-white people and not to the European immigrants (from Germany or Italy) or the Anglo-Saxon American immigrants. This group is likely to have experienced racism as a stressor and this may be linked to the reasons for wishing to seek help from a counsellor. It is not suggested that racism alone creates psychological problems or disturbance, but nevertheless it may make this group more susceptible to stress, especially if it is prolonged. People who have a strong support system, from family and friends, may create a type of buffer to racism. Alternatively, people may actively seek a strong identification with a racial or cultural group in order to create a strong support system.

White ethnics

A second group of immigrants have been stereotypically labelled as the white ethnics, because they are of European ancestry. In the United States, the white ethnics are a large group consisting of people of Irish, Polish, German, Greek, Italian, etc. ancestry. On the whole, these groups have a strong bond with their cultural background. It is quite evident in the way they choose to live in close geographical proximity to each other and continue traditional cultural practices and rituals. It must also be remembered that for religious or socio-political reasons, some ethnic minority groups, such as the European Jews, were considered minorities even before they migrated. This group experiences a more subtle type of prejudice because the white ethnic groups are not as easily recognised. This may reduce the stress experienced by the group because they can often appear to hold the physical characteristics of the majority culture. However, because their 'foreignness' is less overt their cultural background can often be underestimated. The members of this group may be made to feel inferior and helpless in a similar way to the black ethnic minorities.

Temporary residents

Another group which can be identified as a minority group are temporary residents of a country, and include students, guest workers and refugee groups. Students and guest workers migrate to other countries voluntarily, either individually or in small groups. Refugee groups usually migrate in small or large groups, involuntarily. Refugees have undergone dramatic life-threatening situations and suffered personal, social and economic losses. Not only has the change for them been abrupt, but they also have to cope with adapting to a new cultural environment. Guest workers migrate as a result of financial difficulties. Many intend their stay to be temporary but most are forced, by their financial circumstances, to extend it, which creates a state of perpetual uncertainty. Integration into the host culture is not even seen as an option, since psychologically they perceive themselves as temporary residents who will return to their home country once their financial conditions have improved. Even when they experience the stress of readaptation to another country, many fear deportation if they seek the help of professionals.

PRESENTING PROBLEMS

It is important now to turn to the type of reasons the clients may have for seeking counselling or therapy. These may give us an indication as to whether certain ethnic minority groups, for example refugee groups, share similar conflicts and if so, what the implications are for counselling practice. Cultures impose stress on their members in different ways. The potential stressors are interrelated and at times even overlap, but for the purpose of this discussion they have been divided into seven categories: value conflict stress, social change stress, acculturation stress, life stress, goal-striving discrepancy stress, role discrimination stress and role conflict (see Marsella 1979).

Value conflict stress

Value conflict stress is commonly experienced. It occurs where the individual encounters many conflicting values, new sets of ideas, values and beliefs, which are a challenge to their own. If there is no firm frame of reference this experience may create confusion and psychological uncertainty. When this occurs in encountering a new cultural ideology or even sub-cultures of a society it is termed *culture shock*. Littlewood and Lipsedge (1982) are amongst some of the researchers who have discussed the problems encountered by people who migrate. It is important to acknowledge the experience of culture shock because it is a powerful and quite common experience. Often immigrants are expected to adjust to their new environment quickly. However, this is a process that takes time to occur, even for those who are acquainted with the new culture, for example, by speaking the language or having lived in that culture before. Culture shock, then, includes the feelings of confusion and rejection, the sense of loss of the culture being left behind and anxiety and surprise when encountering a new culture.

Social change stress

Another relevant area in cross-cultural counselling work is social change stress, quite a common occurrence in modern society. This occurs when a culture is going through the process of urbanisation and modernisation and there is a challenge to the previous ways of relating to other people. Often people can feel a great sense of loss because the old patterns may be perceived as correct and useful. The new can often be threatening because it means changes; there can be a strong resistance to it. On the other hand, those who are ready for change may welcome societal change because it gives them permission to express different ideas and behaviours. Social change stress can be examined as a cross-cultural conflict, although it occurs within a single country.

An example of social change stress is during the 1950s in India. With a fast rate of modernisation and industrialisation, India entered both the economic and intellectual Euro-American world market. The rapid and incredible increase of the urban middle class gave rise to the culture of counselling and therapy. After Independence, Indian cities from the most western, Bombay, to the most traditional, like Calcutta, became followers of universalistic theories of therapy. Ancient myths are no longer referred to because the clients are mythologically illiterate; also because the therapists are disinterested in them and are choosing to use more universalistic models. This diminished interest in the cultural aspects of counselling may be experienced by some clients as a sense of loss of their cultural roots. It is also undoubtedly a type of counselling that only serves a particular social class.

Acculturation stress

Acculturation stress is another common factor, and an area which has been researched extensively. It is the degree to which the individual has adopted the cultural ideas and behaviours of the host culture (see p. 36). Acculturation can create severe problems, sometimes leading to serious mental health problems. Gradually the counsellor must try to locate where the client is in terms of acculturation to the new culture. Another direction for exploration is to establish which aspects of the old or new culture the client is in conflict with. Culture, as discussed previously, is such a complex network that a client may be in conflict with some aspects of it, not necessarily with all of it. It is probable that some aspects will be addressed in therapy more than others, depending on the value placed on them by the client.

Life stress

Certain life stress events may require a great deal of adjustment. This is of course not only applicable to ethnic minority clients, but to any client. It is an important area to examine with the client in cases where they are dealing with life stress events such as the death of a relative or friend, living in an economic climate of recession, a war, etc. Often these factors are neglected and clients are seen as solely responsible for their lives. We have very little choice about life events and the therapist can be most useful in helping the client come to terms with the limitations and uncertainties of life.

Goal-striving discrepancy stress

Goal-striving discrepancy stress is found in societies where there is a large gap between people's aspirations and achievements. This is occurring in many developing countries where aspirations have increased tremendously, largely as a result of the media. It has generally been found that when the goal discrepancies are high, there is a greater risk of mental disturbance (Marsella *et al.* 1975). Many people decide to migrate in order to leave these conditions. However, the stress usually follows them to the new country. For example, the large Greek-Cypriot migration to Britain during the 1950s and early 1960s was due to the depressed economic conditions in Cyprus (see Constantinides 1991). Many people found themselves with few prospects and emigrated in order to provide a higher standard of living for their families. For many the move was thought to be temporary because they hoped that when they earned enough money they would return to Cyprus. Hence the stress of their home country does not really leave them even when they have migrated. Often this is transmitted to their children, who are socialised to find ways of not 'suffering' like their parents by moving up the socio-economic ladder (see Bouras and Littlewood 1988 for further discussion of this group).

Role discrimination stress

Role discrimination stress is another stressor which varies across cultures. The stress is linked to the person's role expectations, which are related to his or her age, gender, social status or race. For example, people may be expected to behave in a certain way because of their sex, or dress in a certain way because of their cultural/religious background. When an Arab woman comes to England, for example, it may be hard to understand why she has to cover up certain parts of her body which are not thought to be provocative in the majority culture. It may create stress if the woman has to walk in public places where people may stare or make comments about her appearance. This is one of the reasons most ethnic minority groups tend to cluster in certain areas of London.

Role conflict

Role conflict applies to the different roles people have that come into conflict with each other. For example, Ella (see pp. 56–60) had to give up work to look after her children. For her, this was not a stressful issue because her cultural values on motherhood were dominant. However, this was a problem for Tina, a Jewish client in her late twenties. She used to feel guilty for not spending enough time with her baby and described herself as being a good mother at home or other familial settings; she felt, however, that she was not fulfilling her duties adequately when she was at work.

WAYS OF COPING WITH CROSS-CULTURAL CONFLICTS

People have different ways of dealing with cross-cultural conflicts. The first is to react ethnocentrically by abiding strictly by their own cultural practices, and rejecting anything that may be different. An ethnocentric stance may become strengthened when the individual forms strong links with his or her own cultural group to counteract the prejudice faced from the majority culture. For example Lina, a Greek girl (described below), thought that everything would be fine again once she returned to Greece. This way of coping may be to prevent engulfment (Laing 1987) by the majority culture. This is a fear that the individual will be completely taken over by the beliefs and practices of the new culture, losing their own cultural heritage. Reacting ethnocentrically is an attempt to preserve a sense of self that is familiar, and it is common to those who have been through abrupt and traumatic socio-political changes, such as a war, that forced them to leave their home country. Because of the abruptness of events there has been no time to process all the changes and the implications for their identity. When I left Cyprus after the war, for a long time afterwards I felt a great sense of anger, as if I had been cheated of a part of myself which is still left in my home town of Famagusta. Significant aspects of my childhood had been left behind, for example photos, which were part of an external confirmation of my existence. These feelings will never leave me completely, but I have tried to work through the loss by piecing together the 'puzzle' of my childhood years through memory. The body is so linked, physically and psychologically, to the cultural context that it is defined in relation to it. It may take a long time to feel integrated again as an individual and to redefine oneself as a whole in a new setting. People in this situation may end up feeling restricted in their physical and social world, because they actively avoid integration with the majority culture by only choosing to go to certain places, etc. Additionally, there are often feelings of powerlessness in the new culture which lead to a withdrawal. This is linked to frustration at not being able to influence the new culture. It is reinforced by the majority culture, which may experience the different ethnic groups as potentially dangerous, as well as having the potential to engulf the host culture.

The second way of coping involves rejecting the whole cultural heritage, and actively choosing to follow the host culture, psychologically and behaviourally. People who cope in this way were usually born in the host culture or have been exposed to it for a long time and feel that they identify with its cultural practices more than their ancestral culture. Following the host culture is also a way of avoiding conflicting cultural ideas and practices. It is common for people in this group to choose a partner who is a member of the host culture and end up adopting the partner's religion, traditions and language. It can also be a stage prior to developing biculturality.

Biculturality involves actually integrating the cultural origin as well as the host culture; this often requires major adjustments to deeply ingrained systems of thought (Pedersen *et al.* 1989). Still, it can be argued that biculturality applies to the first two groups discussed in that people do not exist in isolation; over time they are influenced by their social world.

Finally, there are those who neither adopt the host culture's views nor their own beliefs nor a combination of these, and have a confused relation to their world and subsequent identity. For some people this may be the initial experience of culture shock, but for others it can be an ongoing confusion with feelings of not belonging to any one culture. This is common to those who experience a traumatic event in life; they begin to question previous ideas they held. During this confusion, it can often feel as if there is little stability in their way of living, in terms of values, ideas, norms.

People who have not developed a strong sense of self may find change more traumatic than those who have a strong sense of an inner world. External events cannot be altered or indeed be predicted in any way, but the counsellor can help the client gain an inner strength to deal with the feelings of loss, frustration and confusion and be better equipped for life events to come. When a client is in such a confused state, it is not up to the counsellor to direct him or her to any of the above ways of coping. They all reflect different degrees of anxiety and conflict linked to a sense of identity. At the same time, however, adaptation to the majority culture can also be flexible, in that a person can change his or her degree of adherence depending on his or her individual mental state and on external pressures. Counselling may enable the person to refine his or her psychological social identity in a culturally pluralistic world and work through ambivalent feelings about his or her own heritage. Acculturation or a type of transition can occur only when the person is motivated and ready; in therapy, this can not be imposed, as it is not a cognitive change, but a deeply emotional one. Psychological change does not take place merely through a brief exposure with the mass media, from a book or a documentary, but through prolonged contact with other cultures and quite a deep involvement in them. Even then significant beliefs from the culture of origin may continue to be held.

When clients are going through social change stress or life stress there is often a period similar to the mourning process; a loss of patterns that were comfortable and safe to practice. Clients have to be helped to find a compromise between the old and the new values; this usually requires time. If they are motivated to integrate themselves to the new culture (or in the case of social change stress to the changes within their own culture) this process is usually easier for those who see integration as *additive*. In other words, learning another language or practising the values of another culture may be considered an expansion of their own culture. Others may perceive it more negatively, as *subtractive* or a loss to their existing culture. For the former group, integrating into the new culture may be a positive and creative process, whilst for the latter it may be restrictive and they may feel guilty about giving up their own culture (Berry *et al.* 1992).

The process is similar for life stress events in that there may be feelings of loss of an old stage of development. The client should be helped to feel comfortable about moving on, but always according to his or her particular cultural stages. For example, western theorists commonly portray the 'stage of adolescence' as being 'storm and stress'. For another culture it may be seen as a smoother process or not even a stage in itself (see Sze 1975). For some non-western cultures, for example working-class Arab cultures, 'adolescence' for girls is not seen as a stage of experimentation with relationships, rebelliousness and independence from parents through travelling, earning their own income, etc., but as adulthood and a time when girls are ready for marriage and motherhood. Even the biological changes that we consider an indicator of the stage of adolescence can vary cross-culturally depending on nutrition and other environmental factors.

Problems of adjustment to changing life conditions are common and this is not disputed, but they vary between individuals. Adjustment problems are real, but we cannot predict whether clients who come from a certain culture will come to counselling with a certain type of problem which will manifest in a certain way. Nor does the fact that a client comes from a certain culture imply that he or she holds all of that culture's views and values. We are trained as counsellors to acknowledge prejudices, preconceptions and stereotypes, so we should try to avoid these when working with clients. However, it is useful to bear socio-political circumstances in mind because it is likely that they contribute to the distress of clients. Being informed about the client's background puts the therapist in a position of understanding the possible differences between them in a open way rather than a judgemental, ethnocentric manner.

CASE STUDIES

Margaret

Margaret, a young Irish student in her late teens, came to England to study. She found that suddenly she had to take on different responsibilities; she no longer had extended family support and felt anonymous, lost and rather lonely. She came to counselling as a way of helping herself integrate her new cultural experiences with her Irish background. She perceived her background to be incompatible with the new environment and was in conflict about whether to sacrifice her course in order to return home. Her way of coping with the new environment was to go to back to Ireland at every available opportunity. In London she formed a close group of friends who also came from Ireland. This was because she not only shared common values and beliefs with her Irish friends, but because she also had a basic mistrust of 'outsiders'. Although she had not known of these people directly when she was in Ireland, she had known of their families and they were described as 'respectable' and 'trustworthy'. For Irish people there may be an added difficulty in that sometimes the cultural conflicts are not acknowledged as they are less visible than those of other cultural groups.

Lina

Lina, a teenage Greek girl, had come to London to study. She was the one to make the decision to come abroad because she thought it would be the best career decision for her. From the time she arrived to London she suffered from what she described as 'deep depression'. She was referred to me for counselling only a few months after her arrival when she was still reporting feeling depressed. She described not wanting to engage in anything and often would spend long periods of time on her own, in her bedroom on the university campus. Before being referred to me, she had seen a psychiatrist, but felt very suspicious about his role. Although I had suggested that she use the language she preferred, I felt she viewed me as part of the majority culture, being a Greek-Cypriot counsellor who was communicating in English. She was suspicious of my role and asked me what my professional background was. She related to me in terms of my professional role of psychologist, rather than as a Greek-Cypriot woman, therefore splitting the 'Greekness' and the psychology/counselling as unrelated. In Greece the psychology profession is relatively new and most people would go to a psychiatrist rather than to a psychologist, so she was not clear exactly what my role was. Although in Greece going to a psychiatrist implies serious psychological problems, it is a profession that is recognised and holds high credibility.

Generally, the sessions with Lina were filled with the loss she was experiencing at not having close family members and friends around, particularly her mother and boyfriend. She kept saying that once she went back to Greece everything would be fine again. Her wish to be back in Greece was evident from her relaxed, more open body posture when she talked about life in Greece in contrast to that in London. I saw her for only a few sessions and in fact she flew to Greece shortly after and decided not to return. This is not an uncommon experience. The experience of culture shock should not be underestimated.

Kim

Kim, a Vietnamese man, was in his late teens and had emigrated from Vietnam at the age of 14 to come to London with his eldest brother. He had many other brothers and sisters, most of whom were still living in Vietnam with his parents. He had been admitted to a mental hospital after a series of violent outbursts at his refugee home. He was given medical treatment and with the assistance of a Vietnamese translator he was diagnosed as a psychotic. He was then moved to a residential home for long-term mentally ill clients. Kim's condition deteriorated during his stay with 'bed-wetting and constant chanting in Vietnamese', which resulted in another hospital admission. His medication was increased and he seemed to become more withdrawn and uncommunicative. When my Japanese colleague took a post at the residential home, Kim seemed fascinated. He seemed keen to make conversation and this led naturally to the designation of my colleague to work with Kim. After some time, he decided to take

Kim out for a Chinese meal. This proved to be quite an illuminating experience as the withdrawn, reserved and uncommunicative man became boisterous and assertive. He talked about how he came to London and the experience of moving into an alien place. He had experienced racial discrimination from the residents at the refugee home, being called 'Chinkee' and other discriminatory remarks. The meeting with someone Kim could identify with led to an immediate outlet of his intense feelings of humiliation and frustration at being treated as a second-class citizen. Experience of the new culture combined with a lack of social support can thus intensify the experience of isolation.

DISCUSSION ISSUES

1 Describe the psycho-social background of one of your culturally different clients and whether it was important for you to understand it.

2 Lack of knowledge about clients' socio-political and psychological factors for migration can often lead to lack of understanding of their experiences. How useful do you think it is for the therapist to learn about the client's culture? Illustrate your answer with examples from counselling or other encounters.

6

Conclusion

Truth is never pure and rarely simple.

(Oscar Wilde)

This chapter is a critique of the transcultural counselling framework; suggestions are made on further cross-cultural research in all of the social sciences disciplines.

CAN WE EVER BRIDGE THE CROSS-CULTURAL BARRIER?

The question of whether we can ever bridge the cross-cultural barrier through one particular method of transcultural counselling remains. Is it actually valid to use a western approach to non-western cultures or are we imposing a Euro-American theory onto our clients? This book examines this crucial question through analysing the relationship between culture and counselling, particularly the effect of counsellors, who are socialised and trained in a particular culture, on their culturally different clients. The proposed framework, that of phenomenological existentialism and psychoanalysis, has its own implicit philosophical base of values and goals. Nevertheless, using this framework means that there is a focus on the individual as unique; even if he or she is from the same culture as the therapist, he or she is looked upon as having experienced a totally unique situation. The relationship of the individual to culture (according to existential/phenomenological analysis), was described as subjective and therefore unique. One may then question how we can even begin to experience the psycho-social reality of a person from a completely different (socially, politically, religiously, etc.) reference system. The proposed model of this book in no way suggests that total understanding of another worldview can occur. There is a general assumption that we can try to understand another person's worldview by utilising the basic counsellor qualities of empathy, unconditional positive regard, respect, etc., a premise in fact shared by all of the counselling professions. This approach opens up exploration for the individual within the four spheres of a person's life; the Eigenwelt, Mitwelt, Umwelt and Uberwelt. The counsellor always attempts to use what the client considers optimal functioning within the client's cultural mesh.

Existential phenomenological analysis and elements from psychoanalytic therapy are not the ideal answer to transcultural counselling. It is likely that the most acculturated clients can gain the most from it. There is going to be a large section of people who may be unwilling to talk about their emotions and work through concerns in an egalitarian type of relationship. Clients are often unsure about counselling and psychotherapy and whether there is really a 'talking cure'. For these clients it may be more beneficial to actually work with a someone who can take on the equivalent of the counsellor's role (for instance, a psychiatrist or a spiritual healer) from his or her own ethnic/cultural background.

SUGGESTIONS FOR EFFECTIVE CROSS-CULTURAL COUNSELLING PRACTICE

General recommendations in the cross-cultural counselling field are:

1 More bilingual/bicultural personnel are needed who have been appropriately trained to work with ethnic minority clients. This is important because they understand the clients' cultural backgrounds and can educate others. Also, if they are professionals they are likely to have the power to influence the whole counselling system.

2 The use of interpreters may be necessary at times, but it is important to train them in the whole concept of counselling. This requires commitment from mental health workers and interpreters to work together in understanding counselling theory and practice.

3 In some cases, the client's family or other individuals who belong to the same cultural group should be consulted in order to establish whether the client's behaviour is culturally acceptable.

4 Ethnic minority counsellors should be used to provide more lectures and workshops on cultural issues. Ongoing training and development is essential.

5 Ethnic centres should become better equipped to offer advice and counselling to people of the same ethnic origin. These centres are of extreme value to their own ethnic group and perhaps (for some) the stigma attached to counselling can be changed if counselling can be located in a place where different types of support or advice services are offered.

The above recommendations would not guarantee a successful outcome, but they may be a way of getting to those clients who remain unreachable to western counsellors.

RESEARCH IN CROSS-CULTURAL COUNSELLING

Although cross-cultural counselling is still in its early development, there have been many constructive changes in the last few years. However, there is still a long way to go before the role and importance of cultural aspects of emotion and behaviour are appropriately recognised by professionals. Research in the cross-cultural field was outlined in previous chapters, in order to attempt to answer salient questions such as whether it is more appropriate for ethnic minority clients to be counselled by professionals of the same background or whether they can work successfully with a counsellor from another racial or cultural background. The researchers in the field of cross-cultural counselling have demonstrated a variety of findings, highlighting the difficulty of reaching conclusions about issues such as counsellor preference or the therapeutic process. Far too many questions arise from scientific studies' conclusions; what sort of measuring devices were used, what language was the research conducted in, of what origin were the researchers and how disturbance or conflict was defined. It is appropriate to challenge the criteria used and the validity and reliability of research findings, and to ask whether these really do imply that certain approaches are more appropriate for a certain race, ethnicity or culture. It is virtually impossible to create systematic ways of working with cross-cultural clients when there is as much variation within a racial or cultural group as between groups. The richness of human nature is infinite. In the same way, clients' problems are so complex that they must be examined in depth and over time.

We do need further cross-cultural research in all the social science disciplines and more integration of the information. Because research has been done within different disciplines, there has not yet been a synthesis of all the information obtained. All these disciplines obtain extremely valuable information, but it only remains meaningful within that discipline because others do not have access to the findings. Instead, all the information should be compiled to provide a more complete picture of different cultural patterns. More knowledge and information is required about what is considered optimal functioning or normality in other cultures, so that this can be used as a flexible guideline. We need to know the differences or similarities in rates, manifestations or patterns of problems/mental disturbances across cultures. Additionally, we need to focus more on specific variables of the counselling process, for example the effect of the counselling setting, the impact of the first session and counsellor credibility, as well as on more specific client groups, such as foreign students, foreign workers, refugees, etc. In the past, research was mainly conducted on the therapeutic outcome in relation to the client's expectations about the value of counselling. More research should be carried out to test the counselling concepts of credibility and giving interaction – for example, does increased therapist credibility mean that the client will perceive that he or she is receiving more gifts, and result in a more positive ending to the therapy? Many other related questions arise.

Another specific area which has been virtually ignored is the scenario of an ethnically different counsellor counselling a white client. This is rather amazing considering the amount of mental health professionals working with white clients in recent years. It is also important to conduct a large-scale analysis to examine all the available research in the field and specify which variables seem to be the most important in the therapeutic situation. Generally, existing research should only be seen as selective. This makes the case even stronger for seeing clients as individuals who are quite unique in their worldviews.

CONCLUSION

This book is an attempt to provide a holistic view of the field of cross-cultural counselling. Its aim is to highlight the issues related to counselling ethnic minority groups, rather than to treat them as altogether separate groups that require a specialised counselling approach and services. Theoretical material and research have been presented and reviewed from the disciplines of cross-cultural and cultural psychology, philosophy and sociology. Finally, a proposed philosophical framework was examined, along with its therapeutic applications.

Transcultural counselling in practice is a challenging and demanding field. Challenging, because it constantly requires the skill of tuning into a totally new cultural reality, along with that culture's own meaningful and appropriate thoughts, emotions and behaviour. It is demanding because the counsellor has to deal with a new worldview and must strive to push his or her own philosophy of life to the background in order to understand it. This is exhausting and tiring, and research has shown that it can evoke many feelings of incompetence and inadequacy (Draguns 1989). It may sometimes create a similar situation to the experience of culture shock. Of course, this situation may occur with any client, since all clients have a unique subjective reality and probably belong to a different sub-culture to the counsellor in terms of age, socio-economic status, religion, etc. In a way, cross-cultural work highlights the issue of how, as therapists, we are not experts in the client's issues. Indeed, with the continual movement towards pluralistic societies we have an ethical duty towards our clients to be as open as we can and accept that we all have differing worldviews.

DISCUSSION ISSUES

1 Assess how you might address issues of race and culture in your own counselling practice.

2 How can counselling be made more accessible to clients from different racial and cultural backgrounds?

Further Reading

Ajaya, S. (1983), *Psychotherapy East and West: A Unifying Paradigm*, Pennsylvania: Himalayan.

Brislin, R. W. (ed.) (1990), *Applied Cross-Cultural Psychology*, London: Sage.

Fanon, F. (1991), *Black Skin, White Masks*, London: Pluto Press.

Goldrick, M., Pearce, J. K. and Giordano, J. (1982), *Ethnicity and Family Therapy*, London: Guildford Press.

Ibrahim, F. A. (1985), 'Effective cross-cultural counselling and psychotherapy: a framework', *The Counselling Psychologist*, 13, 625–38.

Katz, J. H. (1985), 'The sociopolitical nature of counselling', *The Counselling Psychologist*, 13, 615–24.

Kovel, J. (1984), *White Racism: A Psychohistory*, London: Free Association Press.

Prince, R. H. (1976), 'Psychotherapy as the manipulation of endogenous healing mechanisms: a transcultural survey', *Transcultural Psychiatric Review*, 13, 115–34.

References

CHAPTER 1

Binswanger, L. (1968), *Being-In-The-World*, New York: Harper Torch Books.

Boss, M. (1963), *Psychoanalysis and Daseinanalysis*, trans. I. B. Lefebre, New York: Basic Books.

Deurzen-Smith, E. van (1988), *Existential Counselling in Practice*, London: Sage.

Fernando, S. (1991), *Mental Health, Race and Culture*, London: Macmillan.

Littlewood, R. and Lipsedge, M. (1989), *Aliens and Alienists: Ethnic Minorities and Psychiatry*, 2nd edn, London: Unwin Hyman.

Shweder, R. A. (1991), *Thinking Through Cultures: Expeditions in Cultural Psychology*, London: Harvard.

Spinelli, E. (1989), *The Interpreted World: An Introduction to Phenomenological Psychology*, London: Sage.

Triandis, H. (1987), 'Some major dimensions of cultural variation in client populations', in Pedersen, P. (ed.), *Handbook of Cross-Cultural Counselling and Therapy*, London: Praeger, pp. 21–8.

CHAPTER 2

d'Ardenne, P. and Mahtani, A. (1990), *Transcultural Counselling in Action*, London: Sage.

Draguns, J. G. (1974), 'Values reflected in psychopathology: the case of the protestant ethic', *Ethos*, 2, 115–36.

—— (1989), 'Dilemmas and choices in cross-cultural counselling: the universal versus the culturally distinctive', in Pedersen, P. B., Draguns, J. G., Lonner, W. J. and Trimble, J. E. (eds), *Counselling Across Cultures*, 3rd edn, Honolulu: University of Hawaii Press.

Fernando, S. (1991), *Mental Health, Race and Culture*, London: Macmillan.

Kareem, J. and Littlewood, R. (1992), *Intercultural Therapy: Themes,*

Interpretations and Practice, Oxford: Blackwell Scientific Publications.

Khan, M. A. (1991), 'Counselling psychology in a multicultural society', *Counselling Psychology Review*, 6(3), 11–13.

Lenski, G. and Lenski, J. (1982), *Human Societies: An Introduction to Macrosociology*, London: McGraw-Hill Book Company.

Littlewood, R. and Lipsedge, M. (1989), *Aliens and Alienists: Ethnic Minorities and Psychiatry*, 2nd edn, London: Unwin Hyman.

Lowenstein, L. F. (1987), 'Cross-cultural research in relation to counselling in Great Britain', in Pedersen, P. (ed.), *Handbook of Cross-Cultural Counselling and Therapy*, London: Praeger, pp. 37–44.

Marsella, A. J. (1979), 'Cross-cultural studies of mental disorders', in Marsella, A. J., Tharp, R. G. and Cloborowski, T. (eds), *Perspectives on Cross-Cultural Psychology*, London: Academic Press, pp. 233–54.

Moses, S. (1990), 'Sensitivity to culture may be hard to teach: APA approves practice guidelines', *American Psychological Association Monitor*, December, 39.

Pedersen, P. B., Draguns, J. G., Lonner, W. J. and Trimble, J. E. (eds) (1989), *Counselling Across Cultures*, 3rd edn, Honolulu: University of Hawaii Press.

Smith, E. M. J. (1985), 'Ethnic minorities: life stress, social support, and mental health issues', *The Counselling Psychologist*, 13, 537–79.

Sue, D. W. and Sue, D. (1981), *Counselling the Culturally Different: Theory and Practice*, New York: Wiley & Sons.

Sue, S. and Zane, N. (1987), 'The role of culture and cultural techniques in psychotherapy: a critique and reformulation', *American Psychologist*, 42(1), 37–45.

Torrey, E. F. (1972), 'What western psychotherapists can learn from witchdoctors', *American Journal of Orthopsychiatry*, 42(1), 69–76.

Triandis, H. (1987), 'Some major dimensions of cultural variation in client populations', in Pedersen, P. (ed.), *Handbook of Cross-Cultural Counselling and Therapy*, London: Praeger, pp. 21–8.

CHAPTER 3

Al-Issa, I. and Dennis, W. (eds) (1970), *Cross-Cultural Studies of Behaviour*, London: Holt, Rinehart & Winston.

Berry, J. W., Poortinga, Y. H., Segall, M. H. and Dasen, P. R. (1992), *Cross-Cultural Psychology*, London: Cambridge University Press, pp. 356–77.

Draguns, J. G. (1990), 'Applications of cross-cultural psychology in the field of mental health', in Brislin, R. W. (ed.), *Applied Cross-Cultural Psychology*, London: Sage, pp. 302–24.

Eleftheriadou, Z. and Hassanain, E. (1986), 'Students and national stereotypes', *The Newspaper of Richmond College: Sideline*, pp. 8–9.

Kakar, S. (1990), 'Cultural conceptions of psychoanalysis: stories from

Indian psychoanalysis', in Stigler, J. W., Shweder, R. A. and Herdt, G. (eds), *Cultural Psychology: Essays on Comparative Human Development*, Cambridge: Cambridge University Press, pp. 427–45.

Leff, J. (1988), *Psychiatry Around the Globe: A Transcultural View*, London: Gaskell.

Levine, R. and Campbell, D. T. (1972), *Ethnocentrism: Theories of Conflict, Ethnic Attitudes and Group Behaviour*, New York: Wiley & Sons.

Littlewood, R. and Lipsedge, M. (1989), *Aliens and Alienists: Ethnic Minorities and Psychiatry*, 2nd edn, London: Unwin Hyman.

Romero, D. (1985), 'Cross-cultural counselling: brief reactions from the practitioner', *The Counselling Psychologist*, 13, 665–71.

Sue, S. and Zane, N. (1987), 'The role of culture and cultural techniques in psychotherapy: a critique and reformulation', *American Psychologist*, 42(1), 37–45.

Triandis, H. (1987), 'Some major dimensions of cultural variation in client populations', in Pedersen, P. (ed.), *Handbook of Cross-Cultural Counselling and Therapy*, London: Praeger, pp. 21–8.

—— (1990), 'Theoretical concepts that are applicable to the analysis of ethnocentricism', in Brislin, R. W. (ed.), *Applied Cross-Cultural Psychology*, London: Sage, pp. 34–55.

CHAPTER 4

Cohn, H. W. (1966), 'Man as process: existential aspects of psychotherapy', *Directions In Psychiatry*, 6(21), 1–7.

d'Ardenne, P. and Mahtani, A. (1990), *Transcultural Counselling in Action*, London: Sage.

Draguns, J. G. (1990), 'Applications of cross-cultural psychology in the field of mental health', in Brislin, R. W. (ed.), *Applied Cross-Cultural Psychology*, London: Sage.

Deurzen-Smith, E. van (1988), *Existential Counselling in Practice*, London: Sage.

Eleftheriadou, Z. (1992), 'Multi-cultural counselling and psychotherapy: a philosophical framework', *Psychologos: International Review of Psychology*, 3, 21–9.

—— (1993), 'Application of a philosophical framework to transcultural counselling', *Society for Existential Analysis*, 4, 116–23.

Furnham, A. and Bochner, S. (1986), *Culture Shock: Psychological Reactions to Unfamiliar Environments*, London: Methuen.

Khan, M. A. (1991), 'Counselling psychology in a multicultural society', *Counselling Psychology Review*, 6(3), 11–13.

Leininger, M. M. (1987), 'Transcultural caring: a different way to help people', in Pedersen, P. (ed.), *Handbook of Cross-Cultural Counselling and Therapy*, London: Praeger, pp. 107–15.

Levine, R. and Campbell, D. T. (1972), *Ethnocentrism: Theories of Conflict, Ethnic Attitudes and Group Behaviour*, New York: Wiley & Sons.

Rogers, C. R. (1951), *Client-Centred Therapy: Its Current Practice, Implications, and Theory*, Boston: Houghton Mifflin.
—— (1961), *On Becoming A Person: A Therapist's View of Psychotherapy*, London: Constable.
—— (1965), *Client-Centred Therapy*, London: Constable.
Spinelli, E. (1989), *The Interpreted World: An Introduction to Phenomenological Psychology*, London: Sage.
Sue, S. and Zane, N. (1987), 'The role of culture and cultural techniques in psychotherapy: a critique and reformulation', *American Psychologist*, 42(1), 37–45.
Torrey, E. F. (1972), 'What western psychotherapists can learn from witchdoctors', *American Journal of Orthopsychiatry*, 42(1), 69–76.
Vontress, C. E. (1987), 'Existentialism as a cross-cultural counselling modality', in Pedersen, P. (ed.), *Handbook of Cross-Cultural Counselling and Therapy*, London: Praeger, pp. 207–12.

CHAPTER 5

Berry, J. W., Poortinga, Y. H., Segall, M. H. and Dasen, P. R. (1992), *Cross-Cultural Psychology*, London: Cambridge University Press, pp. 356–77.
Bouras, N. and Littlewood, R. (eds) (1988), *Stress and Coping in the Greek Communities in Britain*, REDU Division of Psychiatry, Guy's Hospital.
Constantinides, P. (1991), 'The Greek Cypriots: factors in the maintenance of ethnic identity', in Watson, J. L. (ed.), *Between Two Cultures: Migrants and Minorities in Britain*, Oxford: Blackwell.
Draguns, J. G. (1989), 'Dilemmas and choices in cross-cultural counselling: the universal versus the culturally distinctive', in Pedersen, P. B., Draguns, J. G., Lonner, W. J. and Trimble, J. E. (eds), *Counselling Across Cultures*, 3rd edn, Honolulu: University of Hawaii Press, pp. 3–21.
Eleftheriadou, Z. (1993), 'Application of a philosophical framework to transcultural counselling', *Society for Existential Analysis*, 4, 116–23.
Laing, R. D. (1987), *The Divided Self*, London: Pelican.
Marsella, A. J. (1979), 'Cross-cultural studies of mental disorders', in Marsella, A. J., Tharp, R. G. and Cloborowski, T. (eds), *Perspectives on Cross-Cultural Psychology*, London: Academic Press, pp. 233–54.
——, Escudero, M. and Brennan, J. (1975), 'Goal-striving discrepancy stress in urban Filipino men: I: Housing', *International Journal of Social Psychiatry*, 21, 282–91.
Pedersen, P. B., Draguns, J. G., Lonner, W. J., and Trimble, J. E. (eds) (1989), *Counselling Across Cultures*, 3rd edn, Honolulu: University of Hawaii Press.
Sze, W. C. (1975), *Human Life Cycle*, New York: Aronson.

CHAPTER 6

Draguns, J. G. (1989), 'Dilemmas and choices in cross-cultural counselling: the universal versus the culturally distinctive', in Pedersen, P. B., Draguns, J. G., Lonner, W. J. and Trimble, J. E. (eds), *Counselling Across Cultures*, 3rd edn, Honolulu: University of Hawaii Press, pp. 3–21.

Sue, D. W. and Sue, D. (1981), *Counselling the Culturally Different: Theory and Practice*, New York: Wiley & Sons.

Index